DISCIPLESHIP AND PRIESTHOOD

DISCIPLESHIP AND PRIESTHOOD

KARL HERMANN SCHELKLE

HERDER AND HERDER

1965
HERDER AND HERDER NEW YORK
232 Madison Avenue, New York 10016

Original edition: *Jüngerschaft und Apostelamt. Eine biblische Auslegung des priesterlichen Dienstes* (Herder Freiburg, 1961). This revised edition translated by Joseph Disselhorst.

Nihil obstat: Patrick A. Barry
            Censor Librorum

Imprimatur: Patrick C. Brennan
            Vicar General, Diocese of Burlington
            October 29, 1964

Library of Congress Catalog Card Number: 65:13483
© 1965 by Herder and Herder, Incorporated
Printed in the United States of America

Contents

FOREWORD

In recent years the question of the biblical foundation and the biblical understanding of church office has often been discussed anew by Evangelical as well as by Catholic theology. In this undertaking, the former theology has not infrequently held the view, which seemed scarcely to require demonstration, that the New Testament no doubt recognizes the priestly office of Christ, but no other priestly office and no priestly class in the church. The present considerations have been occasioned by assertions such as these. They attempt in view of these assertions to point out the New Testament foundation for priestly office in the church.

KARL HERMANN SCHELKLE

1 Discipleship and Apostleship

"Follow Me"
(Mark 1:17)

Out of a larger number of disciples Christ calls and creates the smaller band of apostles. Discipleship is the start of apostleship and endures as its permanent presupposition. Even the apostles remain disciples. This is expressed in the manner of a parable when Mk 3:14 says Christ created the Twelve "that they might be with him and that he might send them out."* Even when they are sent out as messengers, they are to be one with him. And if their assignment will be "to make disciples of all peoples" (Mt 28:19), this presupposes that they are to form the peoples after the pattern of their own role as disciples. We shall first have to discuss what the role of disciple means in the gospel and what it involves.

1. In a number of accounts, our gospels speak of the vocation* to discipleship. The most detailed is Mk 1:16–20:

---

* In citation of scripture and other sources, the author employs his own translations from the original texts. The English version in turn translates directly from Father Schelkle's version.

Numbered notes are by the author; those marked with asterisks are by the translator.

* Vocation, *Berufung*, and calling, *Rufen*, with their cognates are related expressions in German, though not in English.

"And passing by, he saw Simon and Andrew. . . . There-upon Jesus spoke to them: Follow me! And I shall make you fishers of men." The story makes clear what the stand-ard for entrance into discipleship is: no human approach and desire, but divine calling and creating. The divine might is first mentioned in the sentence: "He saw." This word must be understood in accord with what scripture elsewhere says of God's look. What it says is that he creates in looking. Such is the look of God of which Genesis (1:3) says: "God saw that it was good." In seeing, God constituted the world in its goodness. Thus God's look is vitally creative. But further, God's look is creative of salva-tion and rescue,* as was the look which God cast on Abraham when he met his test on the mountain—the look to which Abraham owed his rescue and for this reason named the mountain "Moria," that is, "God sees" (Gn 22:8, 14). This is what "He saw" means in the context of a divine call. At first it does not seem to have any deeper meaning; yet it implies divine choice and, as we shall see presently, creative act. The same expression found in the Marcan account of vocation lies at the heart of the account of vocation in the Johannine gospel as well. John tells in

---

* *Heil und Rettung.* In this as in other instances, the more important of which will be noted as they occur, no really satis-factory English equivalent has been found for the German original. Throughout, the German *Heil* with its cognates has to be trans-lated by a variety of terms—"healing," "health," "salvation," "sav-ing"—all of which represent the original *heil*-stem, except for an infrequent *Rettung*, which comes close to *Heil* in meaning, sug-gesting the action through which *Heil* is achieved. *Unheil*, the privative of *Heil*, has similarly to be rendered by a variety of ex-pressions, such as "infirmity" and "perdition."

chapter 1 how the Baptist directs two of his disciples to Christ. And then the passage reads: "Jesus turned and looked at both disciples and spoke: Come!"

The word of the one who gives a vocation is just as decisive as his look, and for that reason it is a necessary element in all vocation accounts. The word is mighty in its effect. In Mk 1:17, we read: "Follow me!" In other vocation accounts the actual word is alluded to with a "He called." This expression is no question about readiness, no enlistment or invitation; it is a command; still more, it is an inescapable necessity. This is the case with Mk 1:17 and Mk 3:13 in the choice of the apostles, where the divine freedom is stressed: "He called those he wished," and again in the vocation account of Jn 1:38: "He speaks to them." The word calls and gives a vocation. The Old Testament often speaks of this word of God's call. In Genesis and in the later historical books of the Old Testament, "calling" or "vocation" means a vocation by God to a commission; in this framework vocation means being equipped with the strength and spirit which are needed for following and for fulfilling the commission. Thus in concluding the covenant (Gn 17:5), Abram is called "Abraham" by God, and this means "Father of Multitudes." Sarah is no longer called "Sarai," but "Sara," that is, "Princess" (Gn 17:15). After the appearance of Yahweh, Jacob will in the future be called "Israel," which means "Struggler with God" (Gn 32:29). God's call evokes creatively what it calls for. Calling is the word for constituting a prophet, as Yahweh mysteriously calls Samuel three times and then calls him definitively (1 K 3:1–10), and the Lord gives the Servant of God a vocation from his mother's womb (Is 49:1). But then the expression of a divine calling becomes an expression of the work of salvation in general. Thus the New Testament speaks of one's being given a vocation to belief, and this usually means a vocation to salvation. In the New Testament God accomplishes the vocation through Christ. "He has given you a vocation in the grace of Christ" or "in Christ," as Paul says (1 Cor 7:22; Col 3:15). Even the vocation to Following in the story of Simon and Andrew (Mk 1:17) is ultimately a divine calling on them through Jesus' mouth. In the gospel this happens as something which can be seen and beheld. Later, Paul expresses the same idea, conceptually rather than graphically, when he says that God is the one who gives a vocation in Christ (1 Cor 1:9; 7:22).

Mark 1:17 closes the vocation story with an expression which unequivocally reveals the divine authority: "I shall make ($\pi o\iota\eta\sigma\omega$) you fishers of men." Mark 3:14 is worded similarly in the vocation of the Twelve: "He made them the Twelve." Here as often in scripture, "making" is equivalent to the expression which describes God's forming the world out of his omnipotence: "In the beginning God created the heaven and the earth" (Gn 1:1). Thus it is evident that the vocation is always a free, efficacious, omnipotent act of God. What our accounts of the vocation recounted graphically, the theology of the apostle Paul repeats doctrinally in the doctrine of election and predestination: "Man, who are you to gainsay God? Does creature say to creator, Why have you made me so? Or has the potter no control over the clay, out of the same stuff to make one vessel for dignified use, another for undignified? . . . So he will announce his abundant glory to the vessels of his mercy, which he has fore-ordained to glory and which he has called thereto, not merely from among Jews, but also from among heathens" (Rom 9:20–25). And in the same vein, Paul says, 1 Cor 3:5f: "Our fitness comes from God, who made us fit to be ministers of the new covenant."

God's creative will gives vocation and through the vocation achieves its purpose. Those who have been given the vocation must follow. The behavior of persons who receive vocations in the stories which we have seen corresponds to this pattern. It is not said whether they were ready beforehand or not. They are called from some quite indifferent work: away from the fishing trade (Mk 1:16), or, like Levi, away from the customs counter (Mk 2:14)—thus even from a vocation that was bound to make him unsuited in Israel for any higher vocation. In short, all twelve are called out of their various chance states of life. They are not men who feel something like a kindred spirit with the vocation-giver or look for his company. As they receive the vocation, they give it no thought, they say nothing. After all, what is there for a man to say when God speaks? This is what the evangelists express with their brief narrative: "Right away they left the nets behind" (Mt 4:20), or at Levi's vocation: "He stood up" (Mk 2:14). The disciples have so little thought of being given a vocation that they can only follow Jesus as disciples in "frightened astonishment" (Mk 10:24, 26, 32). But it is precisely Simon, calling out: "Go away from me, Lord—I am a sinful man," who is privileged to hear the "Don't be afraid" and to receive the vocation (Lk 5:8–10).[1] Vocational psychology has in fact no significance here: there is no place for it.[2]

Now we can properly understand the expression that stands at the beginning of the vocation account: "He was passing by" (Mk 1:16), and "As Jesus came along" (Jn 1:36). A perfect stranger, an apparently casual passer-by, calls the disciples. But this is only the appearance of things. This casual expression is actually of the greatest significance. The Lord was passing by here, just as Yahweh once passed by before Moses' face on Mount Sinai (Ex 33:19) or before Elijah on Mount Horeb (3 K 19:13): "Then Yahweh went passing by. Elijah covered his face with his mantle, went out, and took his place before the opening of the cave. And the voice of God spoke to him." The apparent casualness of the passing-by (Mk 1:16) is in fact an all-decisive election of the divine will. Throughout, what is apparent chance is divine ordinance. But the divine occurrence transcends all human understanding. The human reporting of it, because it simply does not see into the

[1] Paul too will say of his vocation that it is based entirely on God's gracious election. Only by God's grace is he what he is, and he knows that his service is continually dependent on this grace (1 Cor 15:9f). In Rom 1:5, grace and the office of apostle are one notion. Indeed, according to 2 Cor 4:11; 12:9f, this is the way it has to be: that the one called lack the qualifications, "in order that the superabundance of power be God's and not from us" (2 Cor 4:7).

[2] Here, as elsewhere not infrequently in exegesis, it would be perfectly superfluous, false indeed, for some sort of "science" or "piety" to feel itself called on to fill out with psychologizing considerations an apparent gap in what is given by the gospels.

totality, can be no more than a story without a context; that is, in its incapacity to conceive the divine occurrence it cannot present the event otherwise than as an everyday chance affair.[3]

What is essential in the accounts of vocation to New Testament discipleship becomes clearer to us if we compare these with other, similar accounts—for instance, with a vocation account in the Book of Kings (3 K 19:19f), the vocation of Elisha by Elijah, thus of a prophet by a prophet, of a man by a man. The similarities and differences here are significant. "Elisha left the cattle behind, followed after Elijah, and spoke: Just let me take leave of my father and mother." Given his vocation by a prophet, not by God, Elisha dares to say something, may indeed have something to say. Meanwhile, the New Testament too knows of such a vocation account, one in which the person given a vocation says something. It is the passage Lk 9:57–61: "And as they were going from there on the way, someone said to him: I want to follow you, wherever you go. Jesus said to him: The foxes have holes, the birds of heaven places to rest, but the Son of Man has nowhere to lay his head. To yet another he said: Follow me. But the man said: Allow me to go off first to bury my father. But he said to the man: Let the dead bury their dead. But you, go off and announce the Kingdom of God! Another said: I want to follow you, Master. But before that, allow me to take leave of those in my house. But Jesus said: No one who puts his hand to the plow and looks backward

[3] See E. Lohmeyer, "Und Jesus ging vorüber," *Urchristliche Mystik*, 1955, 57–79.

is well-fitted [well-grounded] for the Kingdom of God."
Here it is human will that impels, and not the divine call
that is at work. Or one given a vocation still looks for what
is his own. That is why nothing comes of it. The one who
came of his own will steps back again, as soon as he hears
how hard it is to follow. The other two had reservations
when the Lord spoke his "Follow me." But whoever addresses the Lord in that way, even if it is only "Let me first
bury my father," has lost everything.

The reports of the gospels that tell of discipleship can
be compared with the stories about the rabbis and their
pupils.[4] But the very style and manner of entry into Jesus'
discipleship is basically different from that of the rabbis.
For the rabbis the prospective pupil of a learned man is
the one who initiates the association—a duty, to be sure,
that rabbinicism expressly imposes on the pious man—but
in Jesus' discipleship everything depends on the vocation
by him.

2. Being a disciple is described in the gospels as Following; such verbs are used as "coming after" Jesus, "accom-
panying" him, "following" him ($\dot{a}\kappa o\lambda ov\theta\hat{\epsilon}\hat{i}\nu$), as well as the
noun, being his "disciple" ($\mu a\theta\eta\tau\acute{\eta}s$: properly, a "learning
pupil").*

[4] See accounts of this kind in H. Strack, P. Billerback, *Kom-
mentar zum Neuen Testament aus Talmud und Midrasch*, 1922–
1926, vol. 1, 527–529, and vol. 3, 1–4. The English reader might
refer to H. Strack's *Introduction to the Talmud and Midrash*,
New York.

* "Disciple" in German is *Jünger*, a word that comes from the
word for "young." Thus when Jesus tells the disciples that if one
of them wants to be greater (more advanced) in the kingdom of
God, he must be "like one that is less," the German expresses
this phrase as *wie der jüngere* ("like one younger or less-advanced,"
"a beginner"), and this certainly suggests "like a disciple."

In Mk 1:17 Jesus invites to the Following: "Follow me!" And the Following that occurs is described: "They followed him" (Mk 1:20). Scripture speaks also of "a coming to Jesus," in which this is said of one who does not believe or has not yet started to do so (Mt 19:14; Lk 6:47; 14:26). With John, however, "coming to Jesus" can imply staying with him, and, what is more, can signify believing in him (Jn 5:40; 6:35). Even an "accompanying him" (Lk 7:11) is not yet a final resolve. This coming to him or accompanying him must result in following him. And an outward following must become something deeper than this, a Following in the spiritual sense.*

In their literal sense, the gospels' expression and representation of the Following derive immediately from the life-relationships of the Orient. The Oriental always leaves the precedence to the superior party. Even today on the street in Jerusalem the servant does not travel next to his master, nor the wife next to her husband: they follow at a distance of three paces. This is the way the pupil follows his teacher, the disciple his master. In both the literal and the deeper sense the expression and practice of a Following are full of significance in the rabbinic system. In numerous accounts of rabbinic tradition this order is prescribed over and over: the rabbi goes on ahead, the pupil takes up the rear. "The form is perfectly set, whether the master is one

---

* The author's intention is to contrast various kinds or degrees of attendance (Nachfolge) on Christ: coming to one (Zukommen), accompanying (Mitkommen), and following (Nachkommen). The generic term Nachfolge, inadequately rendered in English as "Following," as in The Following of Christ of à Kempis, really implies a more intimate association than the others do, and carries overtones of imitation and even of succession.

of the great figures of the first century or whether the scene takes place in the third century" (G. Kittel).

Indeed Jesus and his men could easily be taken for a rabbi and his pupils, because of his appearance and the way he taught. Jesus himself probably would not have rejected entirely such a judgment. We know indeed that he accepted the title "Rabbi." If not already at the time of Jesus, then soon thereafter, "Rabbi" was a proper title of acknowledged teachers, somewhat comparable to our title "Doctor." It hardly ever occurs to us to think that Jesus, as one who belonged to a learned profession, let himself be addressed as "Doctor." It was as a rabbi that Jesus made his appearance in the synagogue, it was as such that he gathered a circle of pupils about him, it was as such that he argued with curious folk who approached the famous rabbi for discussion. Let us see the similarity here, but let us also take all the better care to recognize the essential differences.

Thus the disciple who follows Jesus does something that resembles what the pupil of a rabbi does. Actually, however, what happens in the one instance is entirely different from what happens in the other. In the one it means learning from a rabbi, serving him, sharing his life for a certain length of time, until the pupil goes on to another teacher or until he himself is a teacher. But with Jesus it means an affiliation that is exclusive and irrevocable. The disciple who follows Jesus leaves everything behind; and so Peter can say: "See, we have left everything behind and followed you" (Mk 10:28). Here Following is a radical decision that does away with all other circumstances of a man's life.

This Following no longer allows one to go off to bury a
dead father or to set a house in order (Lk 9:59–62). For
one who is willing to follow in this way has, moreover, no
choice between several possible teachers, such as the choice
which exists for the rabbinic pupil. The gospel goes on to
say that the decisive element in the vocation and in the
Following is not the performance of the disciple, but
God's preceding act of electing and creating. To one who
comes and wants to follow but then hesitates, the Lord
says: "Whoever puts his hand to the plow and looks backward is not well-fitted [not well-grounded] for the Kingdom of God" (Lk 9:62). Only one who is "well-grounded"
can achieve the Following. But there is no doubt who it is
that gives this grounding: God the Creator. The expression
of Lk 9:62 shows further the decisive sense of the Following. Jesus takes up the declaration: "I want to follow you,"
and combines it in his reply with "being fitted for the
Kingdom of God." Following Jesus thus means having a
share in the royal dominion of God, that is, in salvation at
the end of time. The same thought appears in Mk 10:17–
21: "And as he went out on the street, someone ran up
to him, fell on his knees before him, and asked him: Good
Master, what should I do to earn everlasting life? . . . Jesus
spoke to him: You know the Commandments. . . . The
man said to him: Master, all this I have kept since my
youth. Jesus looked at him, took a liking to him, and spoke
to him: One thing you lack. Go off, sell what you have and
give it to the poor, and you will have a treasure in heaven,
and come, follow me." Here Jesus has made one of the
greatest possible claims for the essential nature and value

of Following. It is Following that is the final thing mentioned. It is more than fulfilling the commandments, more
than helping the poor, more than voluntary poverty. The
answer to the question about the way to everlasting life is
a demand for the Following.

To the rabbinic pupil, taking on discipleship involves
taking on the fortunes and the life of the master. So also
for Jesus' disciples, Following means taking part in his
life. It means first of all taking part in the poverty of his
life. To the word of the scribe: "Master, I want to follow
you," Jesus replies: "The foxes have holes, the birds of
heaven places to rest, but the Son of Man has nowhere
to lay his head" (Mt 8:19f). The invitation is hard, but
the Lord repeats it once more, and in so doing only makes
it the more difficult: "If a man comes to me and does
not hate his father and mother, his wife and children, his
brothers and sisters, yes, his own life, he cannot be my
disciple" (Lk 14:26). This word does not require the man
to free himself of evil and injustice and pursue what is
noble, nor does it require him to give his full heart's affec-
tions to the wife united with him in marriage and to his
children rather than spend them elsewhere—no, none of
that. But it invites him to leave the most intimate, most
vital, most precious realities, and all for Jesus' sake. Indeed
the disciple is not only to leave all this, he is to hate it.
The one called is himself part of what is to be hated. And
all this, not for the sake of other, higher goods which
would be named and pointed out, but for Christ's sake.
Christ by himself is supreme. Everything that a man has
around him can be in league against the Following of

Jesus, not merely the petty and bad, but also the great and good; not merely what is outside a man, but also what is within. We cannot understand this in any other way than that Jesus wants to say: everything bears the wound of sin. At first this may be hidden. But when a person is called to follow the Lord, the temptation that comes from things becomes manifest. Then one had better see the issue clearly, in order to decide.

But following Jesus, then, in the sense of following him in his life, means following him in his suffering and to his cross: "If a person wants to follow me, let him deny himself and take his cross and follow me" (Mk 8:34). This expression seems to us easy to understand, for when we hear it, we immediately picture Christ carrying his cross as he goes past the disciples on his way of the cross. But what did it mean when it was spoken *before* the passion, and how was it to be understood in that situation? The fact is that the cross expresses and represents the same thing for antiquity as the gallows represents for us; it is the equivalent of capital punishment.[5] In its original sense,

---

[5] New Testament commentaries refer us, among other places, to the *Book of Dreams* of Artemidorus (2:56), according to which the dream of carrying a divinity of the underworld is equivalent to carrying the cross: it signifies death, "because one who is to be nailed to the cross carries the cross beforehand." Or they refer to a Jewish exposition of Gn 22:6: Isaac, who is carrying wood on his shoulder for the sacrifice, is "like one that carries the cross on his shoulder." The reader might consult my book, *Die Passion Jesu in der Verkündigung des Neuen Testaments,* 1949, 218f; or W. Michaelis, "Zeichen Siegel Kreuz," *Theologische Zeitschrift* 12, 1956, 505–525. E. Dinkler, however, in "Jesu Wort vom Kreuztragen," *Neutestamentiche Studien für R. Bultmann,* 1954, 110–129, explains the usage in another way. He thinks it likely that in

therefore, the expression says that whosoever declares himself for the Messiah ought to know that he is risking his life. The saying is found five times in the gospels: thus it must have been very important to the ancient church. We see why: the church understood the expression from the viewpoint of its fulfillment in Jesus' life and saw itself on the way of the cross in following its Lord. For that reason, the expression of carrying the cross was understood at once in the sense of daily mortification—already so, when it is said in Lk 9:23: "Let him take his cross upon him every day." Here too the disciple of the Lord experiences something other than what the rabbinic pupil does. The latter is honored as the pupil of a learned man, as one who will one day be a learned man himself, as a future judge and preserver of civic and religious order. But the disciple of Jesus is thrust out of the nation and out of the world, is despised and hated, and in the extreme case is even handed over to the shameful death of crucifixion.

But Christ's life is suffering and glorification. Following with the cross to death, therefore, promises and guarantees also following in glory. For this reason, what the Lord says about following with the cross fits in with what he says

---

Mk 8:34 and parallels the cross originally functions (and was meant metaphorically by Jesus) as a sign of cultic-eschatological sealing, such as was carried out, according to Ez 9:4, with the letter Tau; before the Exile this letter was written as an upright or leaning cross (+ or ×). Then tradition would have interpreted the expression with a reminiscence of the historical cross of Jesus. A history of the exegesis of this expression of Christ, Mk 8:34, from the age of the fathers down to the present, is given by R. Koolmeister, "Selbstverleugnung, Kreuzaufnahme und Nachfolge," *Charisteria Johanni Kopp*, Stockholm 1954, 64–94.

elsewhere about the Son of Man who, when he comes in glory, acknowledges those who have not been ashamed of his debasement (Mk 8:34; 9:1). Such a communion in life and suffering and resurrection between Jesus and his disciples is infinitely more than the communion between the rabbi and his pupils. It leads into unspeakable depths. Express testimony to this are sayings such as that of Mt 19:28: "Truly, I tell you, you that have followed me, will, when the Son of Man is seated on the throne of his glory, sit on twelve thrones and judge the twelve tribes of Israel," or that of Jn 12:26: "Whoever wants to serve me, let him follow me. For wherever I am, there shall my disciple be. Whoever serves me, him will my Father glorify."

An expression of the same meaning and the same dignity as Following, and already often interchanged with it in the passages hitherto cited, finds its scriptural basis in Jesus' own phrase: "being a disciple." The word "disciple" and the esteem it bears have also come over into the New Testament from rabbinic Judaism. Once again the similarities and differences between rabbinicism and the New Testament are significant. In the New Testament "disciple" is a common word. The New Testament is acquainted with and names disciples of John the Baptist, of the Pharisees, and naturally very often of Jesus. Discipleship means frequently the narrowest circle of the Twelve, frequently hearers and followers in general, frequently in a special sense the most serious adherents. Often it is impossible to draw the line exactly. Between the pupils of Jesus and those of the rabbis persists the essential difference—based manifestly on the preaching of Jesus himself

—that only reverent openness to the word of the law and to the knowledge of the teacher is required of the rabbi's disciple, but of Jesus' disciple, trustful obedience to vocation by the Lord. Jesus' disciples, for that reason, never enter into a discussion with him as the rabbinic pupils do with their teachers in the rabbinic accounts: Jesus' pupils are only listeners. And while the rabbi, as the accounts of the Jewish rabbis tell, boasts of his school and his knowledge and so enlists pupils, Jesus on the other hand foregoes any objective establishment of his authority. He simply claims allegiance for his own sake (Mt 10:39: "for my sake"). The choice, therefore, is not made because one recognizes that the claimant's teaching is right and good, but it is made for *his* sake alone. The choice is directed at the person of Jesus and is a personal bestowal on him of oneself. For Jesus not only instructs and claims allegiance, but also loves (Mk 10:21: "Jesus looked at him and loved him").

Finally, the rabbi's pupil has the goal of becoming a master himself. But for Jesus' disciple, discipleship is not a beginning; it is the fulfillment and destination of his life. He always remains a disciple. Church tradition could not forget Jesus' saying which absolutely forbade his men to let themselves be honored as masters: "You are not to let yourselves be called Rabbi. One person is your teacher, Christ" (Mt 23:8).

As a notion and expression, "disciple" is correlative to "teacher" and "master"; thus "disciple of Christ" is correlative to "Jesus the Teacher." The New Testament meaning of this latter phrase develops in quite the same way

as that of the word "disciple." Jesus semed to be a rabbi
and was addressed as such; so were many others in his
position. But Jesus is not satisfied with the claim to be a
teacher. He knows himself as the teacher—for example, in
his claim: "To the men of old it was said . . . but I am telling you" (Mt 5:21ff). When was it said to the men of
old? It was said at the announcement of the ten commandments on Mount Sinai! With such a claim Jesus
takes his place alongside God—for those, that is, who
understand what they are hearing. He is not only God's
messenger or God's mouthpiece, as is a prophet: he is the
bearer of God's will, answerable for it, at one with God.
For this reason he is also at once much more than merely
a teacher. He is not only the teacher who brings knowledge,
but the Lord who guarantees salvation. Therefore the New
Testament can interchange the expressions "disciple" and
"teacher" with other, weightier expressions, namely those
of "lord" and "servant"; thus Mt 10:24f: "The disciple is
not over his master and the servant is not over his lord."
And in the parable of the faithful steward (Mt 24:45–51),
it is clear who the lord is and who the servants are: Jesus
and the disciples.

The expression "following Jesus" is limited in the New
Testament to the gospels. The reason is that this term is
always limited to expressing a relationship which is continuing and actually taking place and which is not present
except in its very discharge—a relationship, therefore, to
the Lord in his visible presence, in his contemporaneous-
ness, in his historical reality. The spiritual relationship of
the faithful to the exalted Christ and Lord is not described

in this way. The same may be said of the word "disciple."
True, the Acts of the Apostles (6:1; 9:1, et al.) speaks of
disciples of the Lord, and the baptism-mandate (Mt 28:19)
even commands "making disciples of all peoples." Nevertheless the letters of the New Testament and John's
Apocalypse no longer use the term. In accord with its basic
significance of "learning pupil," this term too expressed a
relationship of listening and association between master
and disciples that could be experienced only on earth,
rather than that new relationship in which the faithful
stood with the Lord after Easter.

In Paul, expressions such as "accompanying Jesus" are
replaced by turns of phrase such as "being Christ's," or,
still more profoundly, "living with Christ" or "in Christ."
Those who belong to him, Christ the new Adam (Rom
5:15) encompasses as beings subject to him and existing in
him. Henceforth Christ's people live in him and exist in
him. This belonging to Christ, this "existence in Christ,"
the believer acquires not through Following, but through
sacrament, the sacramental suffering-with, dying-with,
being-raised-with Christ. Let us recall chapter 6 of the
Letter to the Romans. Once Christ was present in body,
now he is present in spirit. But deliverance means entering
into this spiritual reality of Christ and being taken over by
it. This *accompanying* the Jesus of history becomes *entering* the Christ, who is the Spirit (2 Cor 3:17); the Following which we read of in the synoptic gospels becomes with
Paul a shared actualization in faith and sacrament. This
means: Christ in us and we in him.

Now the identity with Christ which is received through

the sacrament obliges one to a Christiform life. That life is first a true "existing in Christ." Existing in Christ, therefore, means not acknowledging a Yes and a No together, but only the Yes of truthfulness, just as there was no blend of Yes and No in God's Son (2 Cor 1:17–20).* It demands concern for one another, just as Christ was concerned for all, in that he became a "minister of the Circumcision" (Rom 15:5–8). It demands the practice of mutual forgiveness: "Bear up with one another and forgive one another, if one has something to reproach the other for. As the Lord has forgiven, you are to do also" (Col 3:13). Being in Christ demands letting oneself be stirred by Christ's simplicity and gentleness (2 Cor 10:1: "I exhort you in the name of Christ's mildness and gentleness"). In general, it demands having that attitude which was Christ's attitude, that is, not having any thought for one's own honor or one's own good, but emptying oneself, as Christ did when he sacrificed his divine state of being and became man, obedient unto death on the cross (Phil 2:8). Even to suffering death the believer must follow the Lord, as Paul must: "At all times we bear Jesus' death pangs about in our body, that Jesus' life too may reveal itself in our body" (2 Cor 4:10). When Paul expresses himself so, it is as if he were at last drawing out the ultimate implications of the Lord's saying about "bearing the cross" as it is found in the synoptic gospels (Mk 8:34 and parallels). Sacrament and life: it is not until the two are brought together that a picture of true existence in Christ emerges.

* "ὁ τοῦ θεοῦ γὰρ υἱὸς . . . οὐκ ἐγένετο ναὶ καὶ οὔ, ἀλλὰ ναὶ ἐν αὐτῷ γέγονεν."

The Gospel of John (and the Johannine theology) often speaks of Following from a point of view almost identical with that of the synoptics. The gospel reports a following by crowds who travel with Jesus (Jn 6:2: "A great crowd were following him, because they saw the signs"), as well as a following by disciples to whom Jesus personally gives their vocation (Jn 1:43: "Jesus spoke to Philip: Follow me"). But how John's gospel assimilates the mere story to an account of faith is shown by an expression such as that of Jn 8:12: "I am the light of the world. Whoever follows me will not wander in the darkness, but have the light of life." Here, Following is transferred from the reality of a visible event to the pure reality of faith.

The Johannine gospel associates the metaphor of walking in light with other, similar expressions, such as the sayings of the Lord: "I am the door" (Jn 10:9) and "I am the way, the truth, and the life" (Jn 14:6). Christ does not say: I open the door—I lead the way—I bring the life. Likewise, he does not say: I bring the bread, but: "I am the bread" (Jn 6:35); and not: I have seen the Father and report about the Father, but: "Whoever sees me, sees the Father" (Jn 14:9). All this means that Christ is more than teacher and master and more than a great, wise religious founder, who lives a model life and by the example of his purity leads the way. He is also something other than a great pioneer, who opened the way to enable each of his followers to go the way himself by his own choice and power. He is rather himself the ground and goal of man's belief and action. Believing does not mean being virtuous like him, but being a believer in him. To go the way and to follow, therefore, mean nothing else than to be united with Christ and to remain in him in life and action. Thus Paul and John speak in the same manner of existing in him (Jn 17:23): "I in them and you [Father] in me, that they may be entirely one." And so the shift in the synoptic notion of Following and the new definition of Christian discipleship in Paul and John come to the same thing: Following becomes shared actualization, discipleship becomes life in Christ. This shift is not an arbitrary alteration of the gospel, but now—after Christ's cross, resurrection and sending of the Spirit—it is a necessary response to a new situation. And if the baptism-mandate (Mt 28:19) demands that all peoples be made disciples, then in future this being a disciple must always be realized in accord with the teaching of Paul and John.

3. Out of a number of disciples Christ elects the narrower circle of the Twelve (Mk 3:13), and sends them out later as "messengers," as "apostles" (ἀπόστλος: Mk 6:7). There can hardly be any doubt that twelve are elected because the tribes of Israel numbered twelve. The Twelve, then, are to represent the full count of the ancient people of God, just as they are to anticipate the plenitude of the future Israel of God, the Church. Therefore (according to Mt 19:28) at the return of the Son of Man they will sit as judges on twelve thrones: likewise (according to Ap 21:14), the twelve foundation stones of the future city bear the names of the twelve apostles of the Lamb.

The twelve are called apostles. According to Lk 6:13 (and only according to him), Jesus himself is supposed to have named them apostles, while Mt 10:2 says only that

the twelve were (later) named apostles.* On the other
hand, according to evidence from all the gospels, Jesus
frequently used the verb "send out" ($\dot{\alpha}\pi o\sigma\tau\dot{\epsilon}\lambda\lambda\epsilon\iota\nu$; thus Mt
10:16) with reference to the Twelve. This suggests that
Jesus probably used the corresponding Aramaic verb (pre-
sumably *shalach*), which designated the Twelve as his
messengers. Thereafter the Aramaic substantive was formed
—by him or by others—and this word was translated into
Greek, perhaps in the church of Antioch, in which it appears that the passage from Jewish expression to Greek in
important matters was completed. The name expresses the
essence of the apostle.

What then is an apostle? He is the messenger of another.
Therefore the Christian understanding of what an apostle
is, is in harmony with the sentence often cited by the
rabbis: "The one sent out by a man is like the man himself." But the apostle is one sent by Christ, and his being
sent goes back through Christ to the Father (Mt 10:40).
That is the dignity and honor of the apostle. In this dignity
he stands over the community and neither exists by the
community's election (Gal 1:1: "Paul, apostle not from
men and not through any man, but through Jesus Christ"),
nor is subject to its judgment (1 Cor 4:3): "But it means
nothing at all that I am judged by you or by any human
tribunal"). His being messenger of another means also
that he is bound to the sender and to his commission. It

* In the Greek text, Matthew refers to them only as "the
twelve apostles" ($\tau\hat{\omega}\nu$ $\delta\acute{\omega}\delta\epsilon\kappa\alpha$ $\dot{\alpha}\pi o\sigma\tau\acute{o}\lambda\omega\nu$), using this apparently as
a familiar phrase without the least suggestion of where or when
the phrase originated.

is not he himself that he has to bring, but it is a commission that he has to fulfill. He has to administer goods
delivered into his keeping. His own personality is without
importance. The real virtue that he must practice is faithfulness to his commission: "Of the administrator is demanded that he be found faithful" (1 Cor 4:2). Therefore
Paul sacrifices his own authority unconditionally: "If I or
an angel from heaven should try to preach another gospel
to you than that which I have preached, then let him be
cursed" (Gal 1:8). The content of the apostle's vocation
and life is the word of another. This word is the word of
God. Therefore it is always mysterious to man: indeed,
foreign. It is a message that may well be redemptive, but
before that it is offensive and provocative of scandal. It can
always be challenged. It is a message and, as such, can never
be demonstrated. As bearer of this word, the apostle stands
in a peculiar relationship to the world. In the world he can
be challenged just as his message can. His right to be an
apostle is based on God's commission, but this right cannot
be traced to its source and cannot be made visible.[6] Indeed
to the contrary. By their lack of understanding and their
earthly-mindedness, by their desire for power and their
unfaithfulness, the apostles make it harder still to believe
in the message. Truly they carry the treasure of God in
an earthen vessel (2 Cor 4:7). So the apostle becomes a
stranger to the world, one withdrawn from it (Rom 1:1:
"set apart for the gospel of God"). The apostle is a lonely
man in the world. He himself is nothing. Mightier than
he, the word to which he is delivered up is everything. The

[6] Not even by miracles and signs; see 96f.

apostle is helplessly lost as he faces the world, "a spectacle for world and angels and men, a fool for Christ's sake" (1 Cor 4:9f).[7]

[7] An over-all view of biblical sayings on vocation is given by J. Daumoser, *Berufung und Erwählung bei den Synoptikern* (dissertation), Eichstatt 1954.

Exegetical investigation of the notion and nature of apostolate in the New Testament from Reimarus to the present is comprehensively presented in E. M. Kredel, "Der Apostelbegriff in der neueren Exegese," *Zeitschrift für katholische Theologie* 78, 1956, 169–193, 257–305.

2 THE CARE OF SOULS

"THEY KEEP WATCH OVER YOUR SOULS"
(HEBREWS 13:17)

The apostles are sent out as ministers of the coming royal dominion of God. They are to announce the inroad of this dominion and to share in achieving its start by expelling demons (Mk 3:13–19). Their ministry is ministry to the salvation of God's people, and in this their concern for salvation is directed mainly to the totality of the elected people, not to individuals. But in the very establishment of God's dominion, the salvation of the individual members of this people is procured as well. Then, too, the New Testament speaks of the apostles' concern for the individual faithful, thus of special care of souls. Paul suffers labor pains for his little children until Christ has been formed among them (Gal 4:19). He longs after each and all "in the heart of Jesus Christ" (Phil 1:8). Hebrews 13:17 comes very close to our expression "care of souls": "Obey those in charge of you and follow them. For they keep watch over your souls, since they will certainly have to give an accounting."

1. Let us picture for ourselves one who has care of souls by considering a number of essential and characteristic expressions in the New Testament.

The first coupling of words which we are to hear and
exhaust in their meaning must probably be this: the
apostle is *servant* and *minister* (δοῦλος and διάκονος) of the
church.* In the New Testament the disciple is frequently
designated as servant of God or of Christ, and a number of
times with the same expression also as servant of others.
Duty and service in regard to God becomes duty and
service in regard to men. This is the Lord's own expression:
"Whoever wants to be first among you, let him be a
servant" (Mk 10:44). The disciple is thus directed to service of others. Obedience toward God must lead to obedience and faithfulness toward others. This becomes evident
in the parable of the good and the bad servant (Mt 24:45–
51 and equivalently Lk 12:41–46). The servant who
watches for the heavenly Lord is also the faithful and
virtuous servant who takes care of the house. But the other
is the bad servant who dissipates and treats his fellow
servants ill. A careful comparison between the Matthean
and Lucan accounts of the parable shows that Luke
sketches the apostle of the church into the picture of the
servant and warns him about faithfulness to his office. In
Luke, Peter asks: "Lord, are you telling the parable [of the
watchful servant] to us [the Twelve] or to all?" The parable
of the good and the bad servant follows as a reply to this

* *Servant* and *minister*: *Knecht* and *Diener*. *Knecht* is simply
"servant," with stress perhaps on the servile aspect of the work.
Diener is a more general term comprehending service of various,
even quite high kinds. The English "server," "minister," "service,"
"ministry," "to serve," "to minister," etc. here all represent *Diener*
and its cognates. Except in one passage, "servant" renders only
Knecht.

question, in that Luke interprets it in terms of the apostles. While Matthew speaks of a servant whom the Lord has set over the house, Luke speaks of the faithful and conscientious steward, whom the Lord *will set* over the house staff; then further on, Matthew speaks of *fellow* servants, but Luke of servants and maids, over whom the steward is set, so that he appears thus to be a person in charge. And when Luke says at last that the Lord will give the bad servant the reward of the "unbelievers," he is thinking of the new community of faithful and wants to warn its minister and superintendent that even he can be lost. The parable is thus in Luke clearly a looking-glass for the steward of church office.

Paul too is capable of characterizing his relationship to the church as that of service by a servant. One instance is in 1 Cor 9:19: "Although I was under no obligation to any, I have made myself a servant of all, in order to win over many." Paul thus points to missionary necessity as the underlying reason for his making himself a servant. But in another place he names another, deeper reason: "We preach Jesus Christ as Lord, ourself however as your servant for Jesus' sake" (2 Cor 4:5). The confession of Christ as the church's Lord calls forth the correlative expression that the apostle is its servant. In face of this one Lord, there is in the church no other lord, but only servants of all. This must be so on account of the special figure which this Lord presents. Paul will reflect on the imposing example and model of this Lord who empties himself and takes on the form of a servant. If a person has this sort of lord, he must give service.

But on the whole, there are actually few passages in which the relationship of the apostle to the community is described as that of a servant. This expression carried still more weight for the man of ancient times than it does for us, because it signified to him slave as well as servant: was this expression perhaps to remain restricted to describing the relationship between man and God? Did one shy away from using it to indicate a relationship between men? To express the reality that was meant, more frequent use was made of expressions similar in intent but having another tone, namely the expressions "service" and "ministry."* A profound saying of Christ's characterizes service as the essence of discipleship: "Whoever among you wants to be great, let him be minister among you. And whoever among you wants to be first, let him be servant of all. For the Son of Man, too, has not come to be ministered to, but to minister and to give his life as ransom for many" (Mk 10:43-45). True greatness in discipleship is thus service to others. It is in this that the distinction between discipleship and world is to be found, according to the broader context of the Lord's saying: "Those who pass for lords among the heathen, lord it over them, and their great ones let their power be felt" (Mk 10:42). Greatness in the world wants control and power over others. Even in the company of the disciples there is a place for greatness. But it is attained in another way, namely by service to others. The Son of Man has given this new attitude reality in providing a model, and the pattern of life he presents imposes a duty on the disciples, in that it furnishes both

* *Dienen* and *Dienst*. See 35, note.

the basis of sacrifice and also at the same time its measure: the giving of one's life. Mark 10:42–45 holds true of the disciple in general, and the saying of the Lord which corresponds to this in Lk 22:26; "He that is greater among you is to be like a beginner and he that is set in charge like one giving service," once more encompasses in its vision special service in the care of souls. Luke does not say as Mark does (and Matthew) that service is the true way to greatness, but, "whoever is the greater," i.e. whoever stands out in the community, is to be ready for any service, however it may be required of the disciple, and whoever is "set in charge" is to be like one giving service.

In the language of the apostolic church the expressions of service and ministry directly designate the care of souls in the church. Both the Acts of the Apostles (20:24; 21:19) and Paul (Rom 11:13; 1 Cor 3:5; 2 Cor 6:3) name the total apostolic work of mission and care of souls an office of "service." The many tasks that are to be filled are understood as the unfolding of this one service to the church: "There are many kinds of ministers, but one Lord" (1 Cor 12:5). Ephesians 4:11 enumerates as bearers of office in the church apostles, prophets, evangelists, shepherds and teachers. They all serve to "organize the saints for the work of service, for the building up of Christ's body." In individual instances, care for the poor can be designated as "service at table" (Acts 6:2), preaching as "service to the word" (Lk 1:2; Acts 6:4), the institution of collections as "service of the saints" (2 Cor 8:4) and as "service of the liturgy" (2 Cor 9:12). According to the First Letter of Peter, the whole church stands under the obligation of care of souls—a care of all for all. In 1 Pt 4:10f, every believer in the church has received his own special charismatic endowment; therefore all are obliged, as good stewards of God, "to give service to one another with the gift" which they have received. Service unfolds in 1 Pt 4:11 as service by word and as service by deed. Whoever serves the word is to know that he must speak God's word without falsification. Under service by deed the letter probably includes every sort of superintending, arranging, controlling, doing good, caring for the poor and the sick, whatever promotes and stabilizes the growth and well-being of the community.

Many passages of the New Testament on the ministry contain permanent direction for every sort of care of souls. First there are passages on how service to the neighbor originates in the service one renders to God. Then others are concerned with showing that care of souls is by its very essence a service. Of office in the church this is to hold true: "We are not lords of your faith, but devoted to service of your joy. For you are already constant in faith" (2 Cor 1:24). This must hold true also for the relationship of apostle and faithful: "Brothers, you have a vocation to freedom" (Gal 5:13). And: "Do not become the servants of men" (1 Cor 7:23). And: "What is Apollos? What is Paul? They are ministers through whom you have come to Christ" (1 Cor 3:5). Thus a community is in subordination, not to its sometime apostles and teachers, but always and immediately to Christ as the Lord. The apostle should not confine the freedom of the church by "tossing a halter around the neck" of his people with his own regulations

(1 Cor 7:35). Granted, Paul struggles for the communities at Corinth, at Philippi and in Galatia. For what does this homeless wanderer in the far-flung lands of the Mediterranean, this beggar-poor man, possess except the communities of brothers that he has founded? But he does not tie the communities to himself. He can protest (2 Cor 11:2f): "I am jealous about you with the jealousy of God. I have betrothed you to a husband, to bring you to Christ as a chaste virgin. I was afraid that, as the serpent cheated Eve, your thoughts could be spoiled and could lose their simplicity before Christ." Paul longs to see service in the care of souls really become what is said of it in the expression: "ministry in the true spirit of ministering" (Rom 12:7).[1]

The New Testament goes on to characterize the care of

---

[1] The New Testaament speaks of right and authority in office, in its task of οἰκονομία (1 Cor 4:1f; Col 1:25), in the ἐξουσία conferred on it by the Lord for the building-up of the church (2 Cor 10:8; 13:10); it speaks of the task of judging (Mt 19:28), of punishing (1 Cor 5:5), of superintending (Rom 12:8), of leading (Heb 13:17). But all this is ultimately service. διακονία in the New Testament is the all-comprehensive, the most profound word for "office." The New Testament seems to be incapable of using words otherwise frequently met in Greek as designation of office (like ἀρχή, τιμή, τέλος) for an office in the church. The New Testament knows these words, but does not employ them in the realm of the church; rather it draws on the word διακονία. ἀρχή is restricted in New Testament usage to the authority of synagogue and state or to the angelic powers; τιμή to the dignity of office of the Old Testament highpriest. The result of such lexicographical investigation is impressive enough evidence that office in the church is an institution essentially ordered to service. The result also makes manifest the self-understanding of the New Testament that order and law mean essentially different things in the church and in the world. Therefore they cannot be named with the same words.

souls as office of shepherd. Christ himself, according to the
parable-discourse of Jn 10:1–16, is the true shepherd. Further, by his own word, he is in his passion the shepherd
who is struck and his sheep scattered (Mt 26:31). The
apostolic writings take up this metaphor when they name
Christ the "great shepherd of the sheep" (Heb 13:20), the
"shepherd and keeper of souls" (1 Pt 2:25), the "chief
shepherd" (1 Pt 5:4). Such titles are perhaps intended to
describe this shepherd by way of apologetic-polemical contrast: he is incomparably exalted over the many shepherds
that are everywhere spoken of in Jewish as well as in
Oriental and Hellenistic state institutions and religions; in
contrast to them he alone is the true shepherd. Early
Christian literature extends the expression when Jesus
is characterized in the *Martyrdom of Polycarp* as "shepherd
of the Catholic Church of the whole world" (19:2), and
in the memorial inscription of Abercius as the "chaste
shepherd who pastures his flock of sheep on mountains
and plains, who has great eyes that look out wide over all."

This metaphor of Christ the shepherd is the foundation
and measure of other expressions in scripture which call
the apostles and superintendents of the church shepherds.
For it is a constant of scripture that Jesus is the one true
shepherd of the church. No one else indeed can say as he
did: "I know mine and mine know me just as the Father
knows me and I know the Father" (Jn 10:14f). Jesus
knows men with that immediacy with which the Father
knows him and he the Father. It is precisely according to
the Gospel of John that the Father and the Son are two
in perfect togetherness. They have the blessedness of the

I and Thou and the blessedness of being one. No one knows the Father as the Son alone knows him from the depths of the one Godhead. In this same manner Christ knows men: from the depths where life originates. And the one shepherd has still another access to men, because he is the one wholly sacrificed for them: "I give my life for the sheep" (Jn 10:15). And finally, he has access to each man from the will of his Father, who supports the world in existence. "This task I have received from my Father" (Jn 10:18). To him is open a profound, a true access to man from that ultimate ground which belongs to God and is God. Therefore his word reaches the very being of man. Therefore man is more profoundly understood in Christ's word than he could ever understand himself. Therefore no one is so intimately acquainted with man as Christ is. Therefore he can call the sheep by their names, and they follow him (Jn 10:3f). In comparison with him, every other, even the wisest and dearest, is only a stranger (Jn 10:5)—if indeed those who come are not thieves and robbers (Jn 10:8). He alone is the door for the sheep, through which they go out to pasture and come in to shelter (Jn 10:9). He alone is the door to the sheep (Jn 10:7f). Whoever wants to speak to a man and reach a man must go through this door, must come through Christ. He must let his thought be made pure and his word true by devoting himself to the thought and word of the Lord. He must let his will be interwoven with the love of Christ. Christ must speak, not he; Christ he must bring, not himself. Those who do not come in this way are thieves and robbers. How this discloses what is in man! What does a man want when he comes to another to bring him (as he says and as he believes) truth, education and love? Is it not true that one who comes to another wants to see himself acknowledged, to gain experience of himself, and to come off with power over the other? Does the gospel not warn of this? All this is in the wise man who teaches, in the educator who forms, in the superintendent who commands, in the judge who hands down a verdict, even in the preacher who preaches, even in the shepherd who gives service in the care of souls. Only one addresses men out of chaste truth, out of real love, out of unmixed devotion: he is the one true shepherd, Christ.[2]

It is with this qualification that we are to understand the application of traditional Old Testament expressions (God's people is God's flock: Ez 34; Is 40:11; Zach 3:7; Ps 23) to the New Testament people of God, the church, as flock, and to the superintendents of the church as shepherds. The resurrected Lord commissions Peter to pasture the sheep (Jn 21:15–17). Paul says of the bishops (Acts 20:28) that they have been set up by the Holy Spirit to pasture the church of God. Ephesians 4:11 numbers "shepherds" among those who hold office in the church, in addition to apostles and teachers—a class which probably designated men possessed of a charism for administration.[3] The most detailed description of the task of the office of shepherd is given in 1 Pt 5:2–5: "You presbyters, pasture the flock of Christ that is

[2] For an exposition of Jn 10:1–16, see R. Guardini, The Lord, tr. E. C. Briefs, Chicago 1954.

[3] According to J. Brosch, Charismen und Ämter in der Urkirche, 1951, 117–120.

with you . . ." The presbyters are warned to fulfill their office "not under constraint, but gladly, with good will after the manner of God," thus with joyful interior sympathy, not merely as if a burden had been laid on them, but rather with disregard of self, just as God keeps his flock. They are to meet their task "not with a mean-minded desire to profit themselves, but from an impulse of the heart." Already in the time of the New Testament a warning must be made against an exercise of office that looks for profit. The warning is repeated when the pastoral letters (1 Tim 3:3 Tit 1:7; also *Didache* 15:1) call for unselfishness in the bishops and freedom from love of possessions. The presbyters should not "want to rule by compulsion" (1 Pt 5:3). This saying puts us in mind of the picture that is given in Mk 10:42 of despotism in the world. Thus even office holders of the church are tempted to carry on after the example of that duress practiced in the world. Those in charge of the church should not fill their place of preeminence in that way, but through the binding power of their good example, in that they are the models and provide the pattern of the flock" (1 Pt 5:3).

The New Testament also speaks of one who has care of souls as the *father* of the community. Jesus addresses the disciples as children (Mk 10:24; Jn 13:33; 21:5). The apostles too term the faithful their children. In the letters of Paul, the faithful (2 Cor 6:13) or individuals such as Timothy (1 Cor 4:17; 2 Tim 1:1) or Onesimus (Phm 10) or Titus (Tit 1:4) are spoken to as children, just as Peter (1 Pt 5:13) calls Mark his son. John also (1 Jn 2:1; 2:14, et al) likes to call the faithful his children. The fundamental conception of this relationship stands out clearly in a passage such as 1 Cor 4:15: "Even if you had tutors in Christ more than you can count, yet you have not many fathers. In Christ Jesus I have begotten you through the gospel." According to this saying, Paul is conscious of himself as the father in spirit of the community. He has begotten the community in Christ through the gospel he preached. Paul distinguishes himself as father from the "tutors," who were slaves charged with the external deportment of the pupil entrusted to them. Paul is united to his community in an incomparably different, profound relationship. The intimacy of the relationship is still more pronounced when Paul describes it as a maternal bond: "My little children, once again I suffer labor pains on your account, until Christ has been formed in you" (Gal 4:19). The first painful delivery took place in the preaching of the gospel. But now the birth pangs persist until Christ has been formed in the church of Galatia. When the church has been created, then the figure of Christ has come to light. Certainly Paul has no thought to derive rights and claims for himself from this relationship of paternity and maternity—only a right to implore and admonish them (Gal 4:20), to take care of them, and to love them (2 Cor 6:13; 12:15).

In Mt 23:9 we seem to come across a reference to the custom of addressing rabbis with the honorific title "father": "Term none of you on earth father. For one is your Father, the Father in heaven." Thus the Lord's saying takes exception to any man's being addressed in the church as father in spirit. And if the saying is preserved in the gospel, then this probably really proves that the church of that time did not award the title "father" to anyone but God. The letters of Paul do not say that Paul directly claimed to be addressed and entitled father in his communities. Rather, since he took such vehement exception to every division into factions, a claim of that sort on his part is hardly conceivable. He uses the expression only for comparison. For his children are at the same time also his "brothers" (Rom 15:14, et al). Granted that by the testimony of their writings Paul and other apostles feel like fathers of the faithful, granted too that the expression became a regular form of address and exists as such even today to describe the relationship of one who has care of souls to his community; still, such a practice always finds its meaning, its value, indeed its limitation, in Mt 23:9. May a man claim to be related to another in spiritual paternity or maternity? Do not such right and such honor really belong to God alone, as Eph 3:14f says: "I bend my knee before the Father, from whom every fatherhood in heaven and on earth has its name"?

2. The apostolic writings of the New Testament declare that the apostle must be *norm* and *form* of his community and of the whole church. We may almost be astonished to see with what natural assurance Paul puts himself forward as model to his communities. Over and over he admonishes with emphasis: "Imitate me" (2 Th 3:7); "Become imitators of me" (1 Th 1:6; 1 Cor 4:16; 11). "We give you ourself as model, that you may imitate us" (2 Th 3:9; similarly Gal 4:12). The possibility and the meaning of such an assertion discloses itself in a saying such as that

of 1 Th 1:6f: "You have become imitators of us and of the
Lord, since you have taken up the word amid much trouble
with the joy of the Holy Spirit, so that you yourselves became a model for all who believe." It is not as man and
not somehow by reason of his own success that the apostle
is a model, but because the Lord stamps him with his own
history and figure. It is not the apostle himself that presents the norm of life by his example; this norm is the Christ
who appears in him. The virtues of the apostle are not
what is to be imitated; what is to be seen and understood
as an example is the formation of Christ in him. Nor is
it he who makes the example a reality, but God's grace
accomplishes this in him (1 Cor 15:10): "By the grace of
God I am what I am, and his grace has not been wasted
in me." The apostle no less than the brothers of the community—all must follow Christ. Therefore those who follow the example of the apostle are his "co-imitators" (Phil
3.17). Thus, ultimately, all stand in one and the same
imitation, that is, the same Christ-relatedness. This achievement of the image of Christ comes to pass with one's
obediently taking up the word (1 Th 1:6), and this has
power sufficient to produce its effect. It produces joy in
trouble and victory in the midst of suffering, because it is
the expression and the image of the cross and resurrection.
It is certainly the great distinction of the apostle that he
represents the community and, in addition, also mediates
the norm of the life of faith. The apostle stands between
Christ and the church. This is why 1 Cor 11:1 holds true:
"Become imitators of me, as I am of Christ." The church
has in the apostle, who is a copy of Christ, its own model.
It comes to be formed in the likeness of its Lord when it

becomes like the apostle. Thus Phil 4:9 holds true: "What you have learned and taken over and heard and seen in me —act in accord with it." Tradition is mediated to the church through the apostle, but valid revelation is represented visibly also in him. The faithful are to acquire both for themselves—the word and the image.

Since the whole New Testament makes the work of God more important than the work of man, we may be right to understand even those remaining places in the New Testament in which the superintendents of the community are reminded to be its model and type, in the profound Pauline sense—though the expression appears to become somewhat of a formula, and then perhaps is no longer grasped in its original manner, but understood in terms of a moral exemplarity. Thus 1 Tim 4:12 says: "Become the model of the faithful in word, in conduct, in love, in faith, in purity"; and Tit 2:7: "Prove yourself as a model in good works"; and 1 Pt 5:3, to the presbyters: "Become models to the flock." So it is true throughout, if one understands the expressions rightly, that in the New Testament the apostle serves the church (and the one who has care of souls serves the community) not only as its teacher and shepherd, but also as its sanctifier; to be sure, he is a sanctifier in the New Testament sense of a sanctifier: not a virtuous model, but one in whom the election and grace of God are diplayed at work.

3. Meanwhile the New Testament also fully describes the personal attitude in which the apostles exercise the care of souls. Care of souls is first a service inspired by poverty. This poverty is concretely described in the mission discourse of Mk 6:8f (and equivalently Mt 10:9f, and Lk

10:4f): "And he bade them not to take anything with them on the way, only a staff, no bread, no pack, no coins in the belt, only sandals on their feet; and you are not even to take two coats." The apostles are little distinguished from beggars, who make their way ill-clothed. Only a walking-staff is allowed them. Even when an Oriental possesses nothing, he still possesses a staff. This is shown in Jacob's confession (Gn 32:11): "I am not worthy of all this love, this faithfulness that you have shown your servant. For with only a staff I once crossed the Jordan here, and now two full camps are mine." The apostles are not to take so much as a travel-bag, something that even the beggar has. They must carry on their ministry in supreme help-lessness and defenselessness with only their faith to sustain them. They are not to rely on an assorted stock of food or money—such as they might take along plentiful and se-cure, guarded in pack and belt. But they are to wear their sandals on their feet, so that they are permanently all set to go farther on: even the relaxation of staying a while in one place is denied them. Therefore it is forbidden the apostles even to give a greeting (Lk 10:4). For a greeting means, especially to Orientals, the speech and answering speech of polite conversation. Origen later described this poverty and its abundance thus: "He himself is the Way, and on this Way one needs to take nothing along with him. And this Way is already also adequate provision for the way" (*Commentary on the Gospel of John*, 1:27).[4]

---

[4] It is not superfluous to note the small differences between the synoptic versions of the discourse. Matthew and Luke forbid the staff as well as the shoes, while Mark allows them. Matthew forbids,

When the gospel and its messengers leave the still familiar homeland of Galilee behind, the poverty and defenselessness become even clearer. For it is now, in the
world, that the message first experiences contradiction and
reluctance. The apostles will be hateful to all for their
Lord's name's sake (Mt 10:22). The worst will befall them:
betrayal, violence and murder, and this with the assertion
that it is done in the name of God (Mt 10:17f; Jn 16:2).

An apostle who has realized this renunciation in every
way is Paul. He considers it necessary to live in complete
poverty by earning upkeep for himself and his companions
with the work of his hands, that he may not impede the
gospel (Acts 20:34; 1 Th 2:8f; 1 Cor 9:15). He will have
suffered on many an occasion and often under real need:
"Up to the present hour we are hungry and thirsty and
naked and beaten and homeless and toil with the work of
our own hands" (1 Cor 4:11f). He represents defenselessness when he stands before the kings of the earth in chains
(Acts 26:29) and as a prisoner of the power of Caesar awaits
his trial (Acts 28:30). He represents the powerlessness of
the apostle when he wrests his missionary work from a sick

---

counting them off individually, gold, silver and copper. Which
version is closer to the original? If Mark is probably the oldest of
our three Greek synoptic gospels, then we may also regard his
formulation as closer to the original. Thus Mark has not somewhat
softened a severity closer to the original—which Matthew and
Luke would have retained—rather, Mark is witness to the authentic
and plain humanity of the original expression. Jesus is just as
moderate in this matter as he is, for example, in the question of
the plucking of the ears of grain (Mk 2:23–28). Matthew and
Luke then speak out of the heightening ascetical tradition of the
second generation.

body whose lack of vigor makes him contemptible as a preacher (Gal 4:13f), and whose insufficiency hinders him with a grave torment which he experiences as a thorn in the flesh and as an angel of Satan pummeling him with its fists. Paul recalls how as it assaulted him he prayed three times to God to release him from it, but got the answer: "My grace is enough for you" (2 Cor 12:7f). And Paul testifies to the complete renunciation of the apostle as he discloses how he carries out his service in all human weakness. If it holds true of the church of Corinth that God selects what is weak in the world (1 Cor 1:27), then it holds true as well of the apostle that he, so far as he reports of himself, has nothing to report but incapacity and weakness: "Of myself I do not want to brag, except of my weakness" (2 Cor 12:5). Yet all this trouble, trouble from without and from within, Paul grasps ultimately as the form in which the apostle's real existence is to appear. For the apostle represents Christ, who was crucified in weakness but lives through God's power (2 Cor 13:4). Therefore it is a law, both for the church in general and for apostleship, that "power fulfills itself in weakness" (2 Cor 12:9).

Thus it cannot be otherwise than that the apostles go their way and perform their service in trouble, need and anxiety. It is anxiety about being secure in life that expresses itself in the words of Peter: "See, we have left everything behind and have followed you. What will come to us for that?" (Mt 19:27). It is anxiety before the magnitude of their task, before the difficulty of their summons to the Following that causes the disciples to doubt and to ask: "Then who can be saved?" (Mt 19:25). It is anxiety before the violence of the opponents, because they who have authority and power—the learned, the priests, the rulers—oppose themselves to Christ, so that he must encourage his apostles: "Do not be afraid, little flock. For it has pleased your Father to give you the Kingdom" (Lk 12:32). Again Paul testifies to the same situation of the apostle. He speaks openly of how he came once in deep sorrow to Corinth. In Athens his preaching had just suffered clear failure. Would it find an ear in the great, rich, luxurious city of Corinth? Thus he was going toward Corinth "in weakness, in fear, and in great trembling" (1 Cor 2:3). Once again, in Macedonia, he found "no rest, but everywhere trouble, struggles without, anxieties within" (2 Cor 7:5). The Acts of the Apostles (28:14f) reports how, after disembarking at Pozzuoli, Paul was traveling toward Rome on the Appian Way. There brothers came out to the Forum of Appius and Three Taverns to meet him. "As Paul sighted them, he thanked God and took courage." Even for a Paul it was consolation and encouragement when someone "came to meet" the apostle.

The tradition of the gospels contains testimony to a profoundly true appreciation of how this anxiety and fear can become a fatal fault when it is not borne rightly. It is to be found in the tradition of the parable of the talents (according to Mt 25:14–30, and equivalently the parable of the talents according to Lk 19:12–27), a parable on the theme of the care of souls, at least insofar as the story can also be understood as one's being equipped for apostolic and missionary service. The third servant of the parable buries the gift left with him. Called to account by his

master, he gives as the reason his anxiety before the master
(Mt 25:25; Lk 19:21). For that he is severely punished.
The parable was then also handed down in the Gospel of
the Hebrews. But this account clearly did not understand
that anxiety was to be punished so severely, and for this
reason made this change: a master had three servants, one
who squandered the property of his master with harlots
and flute-girls, one who multiplied the earnings, and one
who hid the talent. Then one of the latter was promoted,
the other only reprimanded, but the first thrown into
custody. The apocryphal gospel thus tries to assign the
reason for the grave punishment of the servant to a licen-
tious life. In contrast to this, the old and genuine gospel
knows what a fault anxiety can be. It knows that anxiety
can stem from lack of faith and lead to idleness. Therefore
it results in the grave punishment.

Thus the New Testament testifies not only to the obvious powerlessness, but also and all the more to the
strength and glory of the apostolic office and of every kind
of service in care of souls—a strength and glory that are
hidden, but nonetheless evident to faith. In Mk 6 and Mt
10 the gospels certainly describe the outward poverty of
their messengers. But at the same time they state also the
powerful equipment of these very messengers. They receive
in commission the word through which the world's lot is
decided (Mt 10:14f: "If a person does not receive you . . . it
will fare more tolerably for the land of Sodom and Gomorrah on the day of judgment than for that city"). To them
has been given the power to heal the sick, revive the dead,
banish evil spirits (Mt 10:8). Paul too knows himself pos-

sessed of the "power of signs and miracles" (Rom 15:19). He has "weapons for war with power in God's name to demolish battlements, to demolish ratiocinations and all mighty towers that rear themselves up against the acknowledgment of God" (2 Cor 10:3f). The apostle "takes captive every idea, subjecting it to the obedience of Christ, and stands ready to punish every disobedience." Paul has the right to make his "weight felt" among the Thessalonians, even when he renounces it (1 Th 2:7). Indeed, as Christ is celebrating his triumphal progress through the world, the apostle is conscious of being led along in Christ's company, a sharer of his triumph (2 Cor 2:14).

If the apostle performs his ministry amid trouble, still for the same reason he performs it all the more in indestructible joy. Above all, if the gospel, now that the Kingdom is coming, calls to the disciples: "Be joyful and exult!" (Mt 5:12), then this call holds true in a special way for the apostles. It is precisely they who are to be glad that their names are written in heaven (Lk 10:20). The gospel certainly knows of the missionary law that one sows and another reaps, thus that the first generation sows without being privileged to reap and that the second generation is the first to bring in the harvest. But the parable also goes on to say that to the work of mission is apportioned the "joy of the reaper, who receives his wage and takes home fruit for life everlasting" (Jn 4:36f). For now that the one sower has laid the seed in the field of the world (Mk 4:3–8) and the grain of wheat has been hidden in the earth (Jn 12:24), surely every generation of missioners to come will be privileged in some manner or other to reap.

Paul's letters are a testimony to this joy of the apostle. He said directly that the apostle must necessarily find joy in his community (2 Cor 2:3). Trouble and weakness become a reason for joy, because it is precisely then that God's strength reveals itself (2 Cor 13:9). The apostle is "boastful about his community, filled up with consolation, overflowing with joy in all his affliction" (2 Cor 7:4). The church at Philippi is his joy and his crown (Phil 4:1). After four years of being a prisoner, Paul is capable of writing that letter to the church at Philippi which repeats over and over: "I am joyful and shall be joyful. You too be joyful all the time" (Phil 1:18; 4:4).

In 2 Cor 3:4–11, Paul declares the glory ($\delta\delta\xi a$) of the apostolic office as he compares the office of Moses and that of the apostle. Even Old Testament office had its luster. The tradition which Paul recalls does indeed report that Moses came down from the mountains where the law was given, his face radiant with a divine brightness which the human eye could not bear to behold. Now if the ancient service was so glorious, how much more glorious will the new service of the office of apostle be! For the former service was service of the letter, while the latter is service of the spirit; the former was service of death (because the law showed up sin and condemned to death), but the latter is service of salvation and of life; the former was service of what is past, the latter is service of what abides. Indeed the glory of Moses is actually so petty that it simply does not deserve the name of glory when it comes face to face with the glory of the new covenant. When Paul speaks here of glory, he means by it, as does the whole New Testament, the revelation of the divine might and splendor and dominance. So it is the greatess of the apostolic service and of the office of care of souls in the new covenant that they manifest and realize God's dominant honor and power in the world. This office is "service of the spirit in glory" (2 Cor 3:8).

In this consciousness of the decisive importance of their office, the apostles are authorized as well as obliged, when it is necessary, to come on the scene with decisiveness and severity. Christ himself speaks of this in the missionary discourse: "If a person does not receive you and does not listen to what you say, then you are to withdraw from that house or that city and shake the dust from your feet. It will fare more tolerably for the land of Sodom and Gomorrah on the day of judgment than for that city" (Mt 10:14f). Nothing is said to the effect that the apostles are to win over reluctant listeners by a propagandizing sort of gradualism or by actual concessions. It would mean betraying the seriousness of the message, if one wanted to turn the message into a friendly propagandizing for God. The apostles claim to be speaking God's word. When God speaks, man must listen. If he does not listen, he finds himself the object of God's anger. The apostles are not to share anything with such men; therefore they are even to shake the dust from their feet. The messengers do not take so much as a little earth with them, for it is unclean and curse-laden (see also Acts 13:51). Paul too, when it was a question not of his own person but of a cause, defended this cause with absolute severity. In his letters to the Galatians, to the Corinthians, and to the Philippians he leads the struggle against false Jewish apostles with complete rigor. He holds himself entitled to use hard language (which our translators usually think they ought to soften). He warns against the Judaizers, who require circumcision: "Watch out for the dogs, the dealers in malpractice, the mutilators"* (Phil 3:2). And in Gal 5:12, with sarcastic humor, he expresses a wish that the apostles of circumcision presently let themselves be castrated—a remark that to a sensitive ear must have been all but a blasphemy of circumcision. Certainly, whoever preaches another, false gospel is to be cursed. And if it should be Paul himself or an angel from heaven—he is to be cursed (Gal 1:8). Whoever wants to injure the gospel is to be injured himself. Where a real defection starts or an unbeliever hardens himself with bad will, there is nothing to announce but condemnation. "If a person does not love the Lord, let him be cursed" (1 Cor 16:22).

Therefore the apostles have the right and the duty to exercise discipline over the church. Exercise of discipline is committed to the church by the Lord, who says: "Tell it to the church. If he does not listen to the church, then treat him like a heathen or tax-collector" (Mt 18:16f). Al-

---

* Paul employs a word play here which cannot be reproduced in English. He alters the word περιτομήν ("circumcision") to κατατομήν (a coinage easy in Greek which to his reader would mean something like "cutting-down" or "destroying"), then uses the correct term περιτομήν in speaking of the Christian's true practice of religion. The German alters Beschneidung ("circumcision") to Zerschneidung (which suggests "cutting to pieces"), hence alludes to the divisive effect on the community of the Judaizing insistence on circumcision.

ready Peter exercises discipline in regard to Ananias and Sapphira. Ananias' death is a judgment of God, and the apostolic word brings that death about (Acts 5:1–11). Paul closes the churches in Corinth, Philippi and Galatia to the false apostles and demands that the communities do the same. Whoever opposes the regulations of the apostle is to be exiled from the communion of brothers (2 Th 3:14). The apostle also exercises church discipline against fellow-members who have alienated themselves from communion by false teachings (1 Tim 1:20; Tit 3:10f) or by scandalous life (1 Cor 5:1–13; 2 Cor 2:5–11). The pastoral letters are already acquainted with the arrangement of a disciplinary process under the chief shepherd, to whom the presbyters are subject (1 Tim 5:19f). To the apostle it is important in this connection to act in agreement and union with the community (according to 1 Cor 5:4 and 2 Cor 2:6, 10). He warns and obliges them: "Test everything, retain what is best" (1 Th 5:21). But the final decision and responsibility remain the apostle's.

The apostolic office embraces an extreme paradox, an all but intolerable contradiction between the outward fortune of the apostle and his inward dignity; this paradox is the questionableness of his figure in history and experience and the inconceivable magnitude of the divine reality within him. In passionately moving words, Paul speaks of this paradox in a number of passages of the letters to the Corinthians (1 Cor 4:8–13; 2 Cor 4:8–12; 6:3–10; 11:16–33; 12:7–10); thus, in this vein, 2 Cor 6:8–10 says that the apostles live "in honor and shame, in slander and praise, as deceivers and yet truthful, as unnoticed and yet of good fame, as men dying and, look, we are alive, as stricken to the point of death and yet not done to death, as mourning and yet ever cheerful, as beggars and yet enriching many, as those who have nothing and yet possess everything."

3 PROCLAMATION

For its description of preaching and proclamation, the New Testament employs thirty different expressions: say, speak, expound, declare, teach, announce, proclaim, admonish, censure, preach, testify, confess, persuade, convince—among others. If our modern language is much less richly endowed, then this is not only a decline in language, but a sign that we have lost much in the actuality as well. The abundance of expressions echoes the abundance of overflowing vitality in the ancient church.

1. For Jesus and the apostles the word is an important and essential means of realization. According to Mk 1:35–38, after the first day of miracles at Capharnaum Jesus goes while it is still night into solitude to pray. The disciples look for him to lead him back to work more miracles. Jesus answers: "We will go into the villages nearby that I may preach there. It is for this that I have gone out [from God]." In this sense, the proclamation of the message is thus the first task of Christ.

Certainly the acts of healing, which are a token and a beginning of the future kingdom (the kingdom will bring the healing of all creation), also belong to Christ's vocation as savior. And he certainly does not say he has come only to preach, but to give his life as ransom (Mk 10:45). But from the start misunderstandings have to be rejected when signs and miracles take on such primary importance to the people and even to the disciples that the word can no longer be heard for them. For without the word, the miracle would be not a sign meaningful and rich in reference, but a show of magic, irrelevant, merely astonishing. Therefore Jesus rejects the demand that he prove his identity by signs: "This generation requires a sign. . . . No sign will be given it. And he left them where they were" (Mk 8:11f). True, he works healing in the order of Being as a restoration of peace between God and world. But his all-embracing work of salvation is presented in the proclamation: "The Spirit of the Lord is upon me, for he has anointed me. He has sent me to bring the glad tidings to the poor, to proclaim release to the captives and light to the blind, to let out in freedom the oppressed, to announce a year of grace of the Lord" (Lk 4:18f).

Just as Christ regards the word itself as a means of salvation, he authorizes the disciples, too, at the first mission, as apostles to preach and to heal (Mt 10:7f), and, at the last mission, to baptize and to teach (Mt 28:19f). Word and work are directed to each other and together work salvation. According to the Acts of the Apostles (6:2–4), it was in keeping with this commission that the ministry of the word was so much esteemed by the apostles, as the most important part of their office, that when tasks of organization and charity threatened to withdraw them from the duty of preaching, they provided themselves assistants in that labor, in order themselves "to persevere in prayer and ministry of the word." Indeed Paul says, as the Lord himself said, that preaching is the first task of the apostolic office: "Christ has sent me, not to baptize, but to preach"[1] (1 Cor 1:17). By his preaching the apostle creates the church as if in a spiritual paternity: "In Christ I have begotten you by the message of salvation" (1 Cor 4:15).[2] To one who answers the demand for faith in the preaching with a demand for a sign, Paul refuses the sign, as Jesus did: "The Jews demand signs and the Greeks wisdom. But we proclaim Christ as the Crucified" (1 Cor 1:22f). With meaningful emphasis Paul puts the message of the cross directly in opposition to the demand for a sign. For the cross is the utter opposite of a powerful sign and miracle because it is the visible sign of a work and life broken to pieces in renunciation and impotence. But precisely for this reason, the manner of communication appropriate to the cross is the word. For precisely in its visible aspect the word is without outward power.

2. But for all that, it is only in appearance that the

---

[1] For an understanding of the expression, see 98ff.

[2] Paul will here follow the outlook and manner of expression of the rabbis, who speak of the begetting of a pupil by the rabbi, or compare the proselyte to a newborn child (and in this connection the Torah is the means of begetting). Whether the language of Hellenistic mystery religion, which is capable of describing the consecrating priest as father of a person initiated into the mysteries, has an influence here is, on the other hand, certainly questionable. See F. Büchsel, *Theologisches Wörterbuch zum Neuen Testament*, vol. 1, 664, 666; H. Strack, P. Billerbeck, *op. cit.* vol. 3, 1926, 339–41.

quickly passing word is without power. In fact, *its power is tremendous.* The man of ancient times, notably the Oriental, knew and acknowledged the magnitude and strength of the word. In the word he sees operative the will of him who spoke it. Above all, this holds true of the word of the Divinity: both of the word that comes directly from it (thus of the living speech of God), and of the word in its fixed form (thus of the language of God set down in the tradition). The religious man has reverence before the word of God and has confidence in its power.[3]

Not heathendom only, but the Bible of the Old and New Testaments speaks of the efficacious power of the word. The false gods are dumb in their wordlessness (1 Cor 12:2). But God is he who is mighty in his word. On its first page the Old Testament deals with this creative word of God: "God spoke: Let it be . . . and it came to be . . ." (Gn 1). The creative power of the word and will of God continues to work in maintaining the world. The word is the law which maintains the world. It never ceases to be true of God that "he speaks and it happens. He commands and it is there" (Ps 32:9). "By his word he accomplishes his will" (Sir 43:26). And as God's will works in the world, it works also among men and on man. It is judgment and perdition: "I have done them to death with the word of my mouth" (Hos 6:5). It is also blessing and salvation: "He sent forth his word and saved them" (Ps 106:20). This word is of violent power: "Is not my word like fire and like a hammer that shatters rocks?" (Jer 23:29). It

---

[3] See L. Dürr, *Die Wertung des göttlichen Wortes im Alten Testament und im antiken Orient,* 1938.

never comes back to God empty, but achieves and discharges what it was sent for (Is 55:10f). In Wisdom (18:15) it is moreover "the almighty word of God that springs down from Heaven." But God's word—in the Old Testament, at any rate—does not somehow have this force from a magic power of its own, but because God himself brings it to completion. He fulfills the word that he has given on oath to the fathers (Dt 9:5), just as he realizes the word which the prophets have spoken as his servants (Is 44:26).

In the New Testament too the word contains power and might. It acts with effect on man in his corporality and spirituality. As word of Christ it creates healing of infirmities (Mt 8:8; Lk 4:39), and corporal as well as spiritual healing by banishing demons (Mk 1:25). Indeed it bids the dead "with mighty call" back to life (Jn 11:43). The disciples are "clean by virtue of the word which the Lord has spoken to them" (Jn 15:3). This covers not any individual word of Jesus, but his whole work as teacher. This word of his is a power that purifies and creates life. It brings fruit thirty, sixty, a hundredfold (Mk 4:20), thus a harvest that is astonishing, beyond all measure of experience. For his words are "spirit and life" (Jn 6:63). The writings of the apostles, notably the letters of Paul, often speak in the same manner of the mightiness of the word. The word runs quick and free to its goal (2 Th 3:1), and it cannot be arrested (2 Tim 2:9). Of this word Paul says: "It works mightily among you, the faithful" (1 Th 2:13), and: "The word of the cross is to those who are being rescued the power of God" (1 Cor 1:18). Scripture often says of the

word of God that it grows (Acts 6:7; 12:24; 19:20), and
Paul extends the image: "The word of the truth of the
gospel is among you. Just as it grows and bears fruit in the
whole world, it does likewise in you, since the day when
you heard it and recognized the grace of God in truth"
(Col 1:5f). Thus the word makes its way through all the
world and works everywhere and grows in great fruitfulness.
Its growth is astonishing; it is God's new creation. For it is
God who gives the growth (1 Cor 3:6f). First a little community is founded in a few great cities. But the prophetic
spirit of the apostle and the missionary's eye, which glances
out into the far and wide, already sees its growth and its
harvest "in the whole world." While the ordinary human
word can call upon only what is already there, God's word
is capable of calling upon what does not yet exist: and as he
calls it, it comes to be. For God is the one "who calls what is
not, so that it is" (Rom 4:17). It is God's word that makes
light stream forth in the world, as Paul says when he
recapitulates in a magnificent review all illumination from
the creation of the world to the present day, the light over
the darkness of chaos and over the disorientation of man:
"God, who said, Let light come up out of darkness, has
streamed forth in our hearts to make shine there recogni-
tion of God's glory on the face of Jesus Christ" (2 Cor 4:6).
The oft-cited maxim of Heb 4:12f speaks incisively of the
working of God's word: "The word is vital, powerful, and
sharper than any two-edged sword. It forces its way through
into the seam between soul and spirit, joint and marrow,
and judges the intentions and thoughts of the heart. There
is no creature that can hide from before it" (but each must

present itself with bared neck to the blow of the word). Thus the word of God is vital because it derives from God, the origin of all life. It is bearer of divine life and itself creates life. It judges among men. It cleaves sharply like a two-edged sword. There is no such thing as neutrality before it. It lays all to one side or the other. But it judges also each man by himself; it judges his heart.

The divine word is much more than a mere imparting to men things as yet hidden to them. But the word of the apostles is also much more than just a narrative repetition of what they have perceived as the revealing word of the Lord. It contains God's gift and brings it. Thus Mt 10:12f says: "If you enter a house, then offer the greeting of peace. If the house is worthy of it, your peace will come upon it, but if it is not worthy, then your peace will return to you." As word of God, the word is not only report, but God's judgment such as God alone can give. Therefore, when the apostolic proclamation calls the word "word of life" (Phil 2:16), "of salvation" (Acts 13:26), "of God's grace" (Acts 14:3; 20:32), this means not only that the word reports about life, about salvation, about grace which once happened, but rather that in reporting about them it works life, salvation, grace. And the word is "word of truth" (Eph 1:13; Col 1:5; 2 Tim 2:15) in that it creates truth in the biblical sense of truth. According to the Bible, truth is not something that one says or denies, that one understands and knows—this is a Greek-Occidental notion of truth—but something that stands in existence and happens. Accordingly, truth is the manifest reality of man and creature standing disclosed before the reality of God. God's

word as word of truth makes God and world manifest for what they are. It discloses man too: as word of judgment it condemns his guilt, and as word of salvation it makes him just. Thus also the "word of reconciliation" (2 Cor 5:18f) is that word which produces reconciliation between God and world: "Everything is from God, who has reconciled us to himself through Christ. He gave us too the office of reconciliation, because God was indeed in Christ, reconciled the world to himself, and established the word of reconciliation among us." Thus God's action in Christ embraces both aspects, the reconciliation itself, as well as the depositing of the word of reconciliation. In this word God's reconciliation is now further actualized. By being addressed to the sinner, reconciliation is continually being achieved anew, and in this way the work of reconciliation comes to its completion.

In the tidings of the word, God thus addresses man and deals with man. Preaching is not an enlightening lecture on God's existence and essence, but in preaching God's very work is now taking place. And that which is taking place is precisely what is being announced in the preaching. For this reason the New Testament prefers to call preaching an "announcement as if by herald's cry" (for heralding is what the expressions κηρύττειν and κήρυγμα mean). According to 1 Tim 2:7 and 2 Tim 1:11, Paul is "herald, apostle, teacher." What the herald announces, however, is always an event that is significant for the public; indeed it constitutes the public, the realm and the world. It is perfectly right, then, that the gospel is publicly announced. For its message creates the new world in God's royal dominion. Already at the start of the proclamation, back in the concealment of

Galilee, Jesus spoke of this urgency of the gospel: "What I tell you in the dark, you are to tell in the light. And what you hear whispered in the ear, you are to preach from the roof-tops" (Mt 10:27). Thus even Jesus' words may be spoken at first in the dark and in concealment and be whispered in the ear. The time will come when the gospel forces out beyond these first boundaries and resounds in public.

Nor, according to the New Testament, does the word possess its power in some magic way, or work in virtue of itself. It is powerful because God works with the word and in the word. The New Testament says that it is God himself who attends to the word of proclamation and creates for it a place of welcome and hearing. When the disciples return from the mission and report what met them on it: "Jesus exulted in spirit at that hour and said, I praise you, Father, Lord of Heaven and earth, because you have concealed it from the wise and understanding and revealed it to the simple" (Lk 10:21). Thus God himself reveals his word. He creates a hearing for the word, for he himself speaks in it: "At that hour you will be given what you are to say. For it is not you that speak then, but the spirit of your Father speaks in you" (Mt 10:19f). Therefore one hears the word and understands it if he is from God (Jn 8:47). Whoever is thus reached by God's word has been created for it beforehand. Paul likes to speak of knowing how God is needed to "open the door to the word" and does open it (1 Cor 16:9; 2 Cor 2:12; Col 4:3).

The same Paul who in both letters to Corinth sets down such a shocking testimony to the impotence of all human effort (1 Cor 4:9–13; 2 Cor 4:7–18; 6:3–13; 12:7–10;

see above, 57), is the very one who testifies to the all-surpassing consciousness that God's word is discharged in the word of the apostle, indeed that the word of the apostle *is* the word of God. Certainly, the word of the apostle can be heard merely as the word of a man. It is apparently no different from that. But such a view would not grasp the word of the apostle in its reality. For it is God's word and works as God's word: "You have not accepted the word of God's preaching coming from us, as word of man, but as what it is in reality, God's word which even now is at work among you the faithful" (1 Th 2:13). "The word of God's preaching coming from us"—this unusual, stylistically forced formulation gives expression to the unusual situation. It is God who speaks. But the word comes from the apostle. The apostle is mediator of the word of God. And after Paul has said (2 Cor 5:18–20) that the establishment of reconciliation by God is actualized here and now in the apostolic word, he says finally that the word of the apostle is the same as the word of Christ: "In Christ's place we exercise office, as if God admonished through us. We beseech you in place of Christ, let yourselves be reconciled with God." The Corinthians know and acknowledge the apostle's claim that his word is God's word. Paul maintains the claim firmly and asserts his ability to establish it with proof: "You look for proof that Christ speaks in me? Christ will not be weak in your regard but powerful" (2 Cor 13:3).*

* The proof alluded to here and presented only elliptically seems to be based on the parallel between Jesus' weakness, most manifest in the crucifixion (a weakness ultimately vindicated by God), and Paul's own weakness, manifest to his hearers, affirmed by him as a seal of his union with Jesus and thus of his ultimate vindication.

The apostle is the one who brings the word. But God reveals himself in the preaching and is operative in it. This with-each-other and in-each-other of the word and of the apostle is given conscious expression in Tit 1:2f: "God promised eternal life before all the ages of time, but in his own time he is revealing his word in the preaching which was entrusted to me according to the commission of God our Savior." In the preaching with which the apostle is charged God's word becomes manifest, and in the word eternal life becomes reality.

If it is thus the conviction of the New Testament that God's word is spoken in the word of the apostle, then a correlative of this is the idea that the believer immediately perceives the divine word in the word of the apostle. This is how we must understand Rom 10:14 and 10:17: "How are they to believe in him whom they have not heard? . . . Thus belief comes from hearing. But hearing comes by the word of Christ."[4] Paul says that the messengers of the gospel have been empowered by the sending of Christ. As the apostle is connected to Christ by a continuity of sending, his word is so truly word of the sender that one who believes in the apostolic proclamation hears Christ himself.

---

[4] Romans 10:14, οὗ οὐκ ἤκουσαν, can mean only: "whom they have not heard," not: "whom they have heard nothing about." ἀκούειν τινὸς always means to hear someone; on the other hand, hearing something about someone is ἀκούειν περί τινος. Then in Rom 10:17 too, ῥῆμα Χριστοῦ must be taken in a corresponding sense. Thus it does not mean a word about Christ, but "a word of Christ." This is how modern interpreters rightly interpret the expression. Old translations like those of the Greek fathers of the Church understood Paul in this sense too. See my study, Paulus Lehrer der Väter, 2nd. ed., 1959, 375ff.

Christ is thus the object of belief, but he himself creates this belief by his word. The passage Eph 4:20f will have to be taken in a similar way: "You have not come to know Christ this way, if you have indeed heard him and been taught in him." Here too the apostle is no doubt repeating that the believer hears and experiences the exalted Christ.*

The word went forth from the mouth of God and of his Christ. In the preaching of the apostles it makes its way and takes effect. Therefore the New Testament is finally able to say that the word fulfills itself in the church, whereas it was not yet complete before that. So Paul is minister of the church in order, according to God's economy of salvation, "to fulfill the word of God in the church of Colossae" (Col 1:25). And when Paul has proclaimed the gospel from Jerusalem to Illyria, then he has the consciousness of "having fulfilled the gospel" (Rom 15:19).

What the New Testament is the first to say of the apostle, namely that God's word is spoken in his word, holds true as well of the proclamation of the church through post-apostolic teachers. The *Didache* testifies to this with unsurpassable clarity: "My child, be mindful day and night of him who speaks the word of God to you. You are to honor him as you would the Lord. For where the lordship [of God] is proclaimed, the Lord is present" (4:1). When

* In citing this passage the author does not refer to its context (Paul's urging the faithful to leave the old ways they had known in paganism and to begin following the way they have learned in Christ), but rather to the teaching implicit in the expression "if you have indeed heard him and been taught in him," namely that persons who have lately come to Christianity have nevertheless really *heard* Christ and *experienced* him, even though he was not to be seen or heard in any *human* way.

the *Didache* speaks of the teachers of the church, it means
no longer the generation of the first apostles, but the later
apostles, prophets and teachers. In preaching, they speak
the word of God. And where God's being Lord is proclaimed, he himself is there. In last analysis this is also
the justification and basis of the extraordinary claim we
make today when we characterize our unassuming preaching as proclamation of the word of God, indeed as word
of God itself, and therefore demand a hearing for this
word.

Finally, may we ask how it is to come to pass that God
work in the word of a man and make it into his own? We
can compare what comes to pass here with what comes to
pass in a sacrament: in doing so we certainly cannot explain
either the one event or the other. Just as the natural cleansing power of water becomes efficacious beyond all the power
of nature by the touch of God's finger in baptism, God's
will makes the cleansing and vivifying power that dwells
naturally in the word efficacious beyond all the power of
nature. This comparison to a sacrament holds true for the
word, therefore, insofar as the word does not work magic-
ally—as if it were some sort of charm. A sacrament works
only where it is received in faith, and likewise the word
works only where it is heard in faith. The word is honored
and is realized as the sacrament is. It works in what objec-
tively comes to pass. Using Augustine's formulation and
extending it, one frequently designates the sacrament as
verbum visibile (Augustine, *PL* 35:1840 and 42:356f),
the word as *sacramentum audibile* (see *ibid.* 37:969).
Paschasius Radbertus, the authoritative theologian of his

time in sacramental doctrine, can say, in the terminology of the ninth century: *Est autem sacramentus et in scripturis divinis, ubicumque sacer spiritus in eisdem interius aliquid efficaciter loquendo operatur* (PL 120:1275f: "There is a sacrament in sacred scriptures as well, wherever the Holy Spirit works in them efficaciously speaking something within [us]").

Even today the church knows and still speaks of this salutary power of the word. In the Ambrosian liturgy the priest says before the reading of the epistle: *Apostolica doctrina repleat nos gratia divina* (May the teaching of the apostle fill us with divine grace). And in the Roman liturgy the proclamation of the gospel closes with the blessing: *Per evangelica dicta deleantur nostra delicta* (May our negligences be wiped out by the words of the gospel). But more, the proclamation of the word in the expository sermon has the power of reconciliation. Hence the practice of offering a prayer for forgiveness of sins over the community after the sermon. And the *Pontificale Romanum* says in the ordination of subdeacon and deacon: *Accipite potestatem legendi epistolas, protestatem legendi evangelium in ecclesia Dei tam pro visis quam pro defunctis* (Receive the power of reading the epistle, the power of reading the gospel in the church of God, for the living as well as for the dead). If need be, the word "pro" in the phrase "pro vivis" could be understood in the moral sense, so that the gospel would be supposed to apply to the living and to put them in mind of their duty; but the "pro" in "pro defunctis" can in no wise be so meant, and thus the consecration formula can be saying only that the gospel works blessing and salvation for the living as well as for the dead.

3. The word of God urges toward realization, toward begetting of life, toward establishment of a hearing community. Therefore wherever the word of God is, there is always church. The word creates church. It creates the start of the church in first bringing about the division between believers and nonbelievers. Preaching brings it about "that they look and do not see, hear and do not understand" (Mk 4:12; compare Jn 7:43; Acts 14:14f; 2 Cor 2:15f). Therefore the word gathers the church together by bringing vocation.* Indeed the faithful are the "recipients of God's vocation" (Rom 1:6; 1 Cor 1:24; Heb 9:15). But the call of God resounds audibly here and now by the word of the message. If, according to 2 Cor 3:6, preaching "is service of the new covenant," it is so, surely, because proclamation continues to shape the new covenant, the church. In his address in Miletus to the presbyters from Ephesus, Paul therefore says: "I recommend you to God and to the word of his grace, which word has power to erect the edifice and to bestow the inheritance among all his saints" (Acts 20:32). The word erects the church here and now and completes it even for reception of the inheritance.

Hence it is in the word that the church is constantly purified, strengthened, renewed and shaped anew—insofar as this word is proclaimed as admonition and command. Directed at the believer as a demand, it first becomes a judgment for him, but subsequently becomes a new form for his life. This exhortatory word is spoken in the New Testa-

* Vocation (see 9, note) is fundamentally a call. The church appears on the scene preaching—proclaiming—the gospel. This event effects the division of society into those who will not hear the proclamation and those who will; the latter, then, are the church, the elect, the called, the recipients of vocation.

ment not simply to the man, but to the New Man freed from sin and death. He is called upon in the admonition to provide a place of welcome for the life bestowed on him and to become that which he is. In this way Rom 6 admonishes: you have perished to sin. So put sin to death in your body and live for justice! Since the word as God's word is creative here too, it does not merely demand what the admonition announces, but at the same times realizes it. As the demand confronts the believer, the divine power of the word at the same time stirs him. Therefore the admonitions are not merely commands, but already glad tidings. In this the command loses nothing of its severity and its seriousness. Rather this holds true: "With fear and trembling work your salvation. For it is God who works in you" (Phil 2:12f). The redeemed is not to forget one moment that he is never alone, for God stands over him and works together with him. Should he wish to oppose the workings of this God, he must be burned to ashes at his holy proximity. So he must always adapt himself to the working of God. Being aware of God and his working thus does not release the man from his responsibility, but binds him fast in fear and trembling to the severest responsibility.

The proclaimed word creates the church not with a force that cannot fail, but only where it is heard and accepted. Hearing is genuine only where hearing becomes obeying (from ἀκούειν comes ὑπακοή).* The church's being in highest

* "Hearing" (hören) becomes "obeying" (gehorchen). An interrelation of the words for hearing and obeying is much more obvious in German or Greek or even Latin (oboedire, the source of the English "obey," derives rrom ob and audire) than it is in English. English takes "hearken" from "hear" as German takes horchen from hören, but does not go on to take "obey" (gehorchen) from "hearken" or "obedient" (gehorsam) from "hear."

measure a religion of hearing and obeying constitutes precisely the essence of Old and New Testament belief and distinguishes it from every other kind of religiosity, which always desires to have intuition of the Godhead and hopes by intuition to attain salvation. Therefore Paul can describe the situation of the Christian simply as "obedience of faith" (Rom 1:5; Gal 3:2), that is, as a hearing and obeying that consists in faith, and a faith that is present in hearing and obeying. And according to 1 Pt 1:14, the Christians have become "like children by obedience."

The word creates for itself its community. It has its power from him and in him by whom it has been sent—and it still abides in him when it is released by him. Of this sending is said: "How are they to believe in one whom they have not heard? How are they to hear him without a herald? How are heralds to proclaim unless they have been sent?" (Rom 10:14f). Thus it was necessary that the heralds be sent. Sent by whom? Their sending has a double origin, a more immediate and a more remote.

In a more immediate way the heralds of the word have been sent by the church, from out of its communion and tradition. It lives on the word and releases from its life a new life-creating word. But a church that wants to send, found and testify must possess the full certainty and power of its existence—naturally not of itself, but because God's power completes itself in weakness—that its messengers, too, may be in full possession of power. Therefore it must be a church clear and true in belief and teaching, in order that the messengers, relying on tradition, may receive from the Lord that gospel which they have to hand on faithfully in their turn (1 Cor 11:23; 15:3). In the concrete word of the church, tradition is brought to account as address to the hearer. In this way and not in some kind of poetic recall or reconstruction by research, the salvation history is made presently relevant. When tradition addresses itself to men, salvation history reaches expression in word, and in word it achieves realization.

Certainty of belief and teaching demands that the proclamation of the church sound the same note throughout successive times and over the whole of the community at any given moment. In connection with his command that women keep silence in the assembly, Paul reproaches the Corinthians: "Now, is the word of God something derived from you, or is it something received by all of you?" (1 Cor 14:36). The older tradition of the earlier community is thus norm for the later. If the word had been derived from the Corinthians, then they might have been able to shape their own customs. But as it is they stand in dependence on the larger and older church. The older church becomes the rule of the younger, no doubt because the word in its first realization creates for itself with original power and authoritative certainty the pattern that is appropriate to its own essence and valid for other instances. This arrangement of things is acknowledged by the younger church when the church of Antioch sends Paul, Barnabas and others to Jerusalem in order to obtain from there the solution to a conflict (Acts 15:2). But the elder apostles do not give a command like a governing board; they offer a brotherly piece of advice: "If you do that, then you are acting properly" (Acts 15:29).

Thus valid preaching exists only in and through the

church. Only where there is a church is the true word spoken and heard. Therefore it may well be possible or necessary at some time to condemn and reform uses or abuses of the church by recalling the biblical word and using it as a norm. But it is not possible for an individual to appeal to the gospel alone, as it were, against the whole church of all times and places.

Thus the heralds of the word (Rom 10:14f) receive their mission most immediately from the communion of the church. In propagating the church's word they extend it beyond the boundaries that the church has known up to this time and find it a larger and broader place of welcome. But behind the sending by the church extends a further vista, the sending through Christ and in Christ by the Father down to us. The apostles of the church have been sent out by Christ. But he himself has been sent by the Father (Lk 4:18; Jn 5:36). From being sent by the Father to us he himself sends the apostles out (Mt 10:40; Jn 17:18). This sending goes forward for an incalculable distance, reaching all men and even the boundaries of world and time (Mt 28:19f). It is a *single* series of sendings that leads from the eternity of God into time and reaches back from time into eternity. Whoever hears the apostle aright and joins him in accepting the message—Christ reaches him and with Christ, the Father.

The word that creates the church we understand first of all as preaching. But it is more than this. For the word is spoken in the church in a multitude of ways. It is the word which combines with the church's actions and gives them meaning, thus reveals God's working and, indeed, effects it:

this is the word in which *sacrament* is administered. According to the order instituted by the New Testament, word and sacrament are a unity. *The baptism-mandate* which the church has received from the glorified Lord unites the action with the accomplishing and teaching word (Mt 28:19f). Also according to the teaching of the apostles, sign and word belong to baptism. So it is when Eph 5:26 says of baptism that Christ "sanctifies the church in cleansing it by the bath of water in the word." The word is so essential to the action that the cleansing and sanctifying work of the action is ascribed to the word. As the word in the baptismal action awards salvation and life to the one baptized, it actually brings the gifts which it names. According to 1 Pt 3:21: "That baptism saves which is not a washing of the soiled body, but a prayer to God for a good conscience in virtue of the resurrection of Christ." The bath of baptism is not an outward washing of the body, but an inward, moral-spiritual cleansing. It receives this power from the resurrection of Christ. The spirituality and inwardness of the proceeding is produced by the word spoken in the action, because the word is always a deeply spiritual happening. Here this word is the prayer spoken in the rite, a plea for a good conscience, thus for an inward accomplishment of what is happening outwardly in the washing. God will surely fulfill the prayer and by his action bestow a cleanness and goodness of the inner man on the one baptized. God makes the word efficacious. *The imposition of hands* mediates the gifts of the spirit to the baptized (Acts 8:15–17), just as it mediates the sending which confers office on ministers of the church (Acts 6:6; 13:3; 14:23; 1 Tim 4:14). But the former imposition of hands as well as the latter takes place (according to the testimonies cited) with a word that both instructs and pleads, with "prophecy" and "intercession." *In the communion of the supper, the word,* which recounts the redeeming sacrifice of the Lord and in doing so interprets the sign of bread and wine, brings with it the death of the Lord for a continual renewing of the salvation event. Word and sign together make of this sacrament the "proclamation of the death of the Lord" (I Cor 11:26). Here Paul designates the sacrament with the same expression with which he otherwise frequently designates preaching. Sacrament is correlated to proclamation of the word, can indeed even be considered a special sort of proclamation. Sacrament has ultimately a proclamation-character, while word has a sacrament-character.[5]

Of this word which in coming to meet the material element creates sacrament—of this word may be said once more and with yet deeper meaning, that it does not recount only a past event of salvation. Here it is itself a redeeming and saving reality. The history which the gospel narrates becomes in the cultic mystery *present*. When read and preached in the divine service, the written gospel becomes a word that lives, a word of God that is at work. Arranged in the full progression of the church year, the gospels make present, they complete, they extend Christ's whole work of salvation—incarnation, death, exaltation—to the believer who hears them spoken.

4. The New Testament speaks finally of the *minister of*

[5] On the manifoldness of the word in the church, see D. Barsotti, *Christliches Mysterium und Wort Gottes,* 1957; H. Schlier, *Wort Gottes, eine neutestamentliche Besinnung,* 1958.

the word, his equipping, and his exercise of the ministry. The New Testament is firmly stamped with the tradition that Jesus sent his disciples out not singly, but two by two. Therefore it doubles its account of this, at Mk 6:7 on the occasion of the mission of the Twelve, and at Lk 10:1 on the occasion of the mission of the seventy-two disciples. It is clear what this means. Communion is to give the messengers human security. Two men can help each other, support and guard each other. But this "two by two" is also destined to give security to the message. If personal genius were what mattered, an individual left to himself might be capable of delivering the proclamation. Yet precisely this is not required: what is required is faithfulness to the assigned message. The message is guaranteed by this, that two keep each other in mind of it and vouch for each other in its preaching. The apostles need not be philosophers, not learned men, not skilled orators who might be capable of captivating men with their own word. According to Acts 4:13, they are men without any learned formation. In 1 Cor 1:18–25, Paul warns against the desire for brilliance in a philosophic style of address, such as that of Apollos. For there is danger that the folly of the cross will be hidden by it. Paul himself has no skill at oratory (2 Cor 11:6: "I am no professional orator"). The word comes provided for the apostle's preaching. In proclaiming it he has only to do his service to it. He is not lord, but "minister of the gospel" (Col 1:23; Eph 3:7) and "minister of the word" (Lk 1:2; Acts 6:4).

Nor do extraordinary things such as speaking with tongues or ecstasy matter. Paul thanks God that he has these gifts: "I thank God that I surpass you all in talking with tongues" (1 Cor 14:18). But the belief that God's word is to be found in a special manner in ecstatic address Paul sharply opposes. He puts limits on the use of enraptured talk in the church and forces it into second place after meaningful expression: "In the church I should rather deliver five words with understanding and thereby teach others too, than ten thousand words in the rapture of talking with tongues" (1 Cor 14:19).

Ultimately even the personal motives of the preacher do not matter. As early as New Testament times, something must be said of humanly inadequate motives for proclamation: "Various persons proclaim Christ from envy or contentiousness, but others from a good disposition. . . . So what? If only—in all ways, whether in outward show or in reality—Christ be proclaimed" (Phil 1:15–18). Even by a sermon given from mixed motives those who hear it can be won over to faith.

Now if the religious or ethical personality of the preacher is not decisive for the efficaciousness of the word, precisely because the word works not from the strength of man but from the strength of God, nevertheless there still exists for the preacher the duty to carry on his activity with an attitude appropriate to the word. From faithfulness in ministry of the word it necessarily follows that certain things are bidden him and other things forbidden him. Faithfulness of service forbids any sort of "falsifying" (2 Cor 4:2) the word, or "driving bargains and petty deals with the word, as many do" (2 Cor 2:17). False teachers, to be sure, who give the lie to the scandal of the cross with their pretty talk, "trick the hearts of the guileless with flattering talk and well-formed speech" (Rom 16:18). And so the preacher must guard against the temptation to proclaim the word for his own advantage, for gain of money or honor (1 Th 2:4; 2 Cor 12:13; 1 Pt 5:2). He is positively bound, immediately and in all he does, by the principle that the honor of God can tolerate no conflict between the words and the life of the preacher—such a conflict as exists, for example, with the Judaizing missionaries: "You teach the other person, but do you teach yourself? You that proclaim, No stealing: do you not steal? You that say, No adultery: do you not commit adultery?" (Rom 2:21–24). Paul warns the presbyters (Acts 20:28) that they are to look out for themselves as well as for their flock. Faithful proclamation especially demands openness, clarity and truth of speech (how often Paul calls for just this: 1 Th 2:3f; 2 Cor 1:14; 2:17; 4:2; 5:11; 13:8, etc.). The preacher must "go straight in keeping with the truth of the gospel" (Gal 2:14). Let him be the unmixed Yes, just as Christ is the pure Yes to God's promises (2 Cor 1:19). But above all it is certain he must see that no one can accomplish anything if he acts in opposition to the truth; one can only serve the truth (2 Cor 13:8). Openness of speech comes to light in that "frankness to say anything" ($\pi\alpha\rho\rho\eta\sigma\iota\alpha$) which the New Testament demands over and over again (Acts 4:29; 2 Cor 3:12; Eph 3:12; Phil 1:20; Heb 4:16). It is frankness before men to deliver the message uncurtailed before the world, as it is also confidence and certainty before God to feel privileged to say anything before him and to him. The apostolic letters go on in their demands: the proclamation must not take place with empty words, but issue from the power of God (1 Cor 4:20: "The Kingdom of God does not consist in word but in power"). The word must be spoken from a confident heart (2 Cor 5:6, 8: "Therefore we are confident all the time"). It must be spoken from faith (2 Cor 4:13: "But because we have the same spirit of faith of which it is said, *I believe, therefore I speak,* so we believe, and therefore we speak too"). It must be spoken from the spirit, to men filled with the spirit (1 Cor 2:13: "Of this we do not speak with words taught by human wisdom, but with words taught by the spirit, in that we interpret what is of the spirit to those who are of the spirit"). The word so needs to be brought to the church in love that the minister of the word must offer himself at the same time as he offers the gospel (1 Th 2:7f: "As when a mother cherishes her children, so attached were we to you in our heart that we wanted you to share not only the gospel of God but also our heart. For you had become dear to us"). The apostle is not only teacher; he is caretaker of the gospel, offering priestly sacrifice in its proclamation and offering himself along with it (Rom 15:16; Phil 2:17. See also 122ff). But, as the situation stands, none of this is demanded of the preacher for the sake of the word of God, as if the word were in any way dependent on it—God can always raise up children to Abraham from the very stones—but it is for the sake of the preacher himself, lest while preaching to others he himself be lost (1 Cor 9:27).

Yet the word in the church is not the charge merely of special office holders. All must be concerned for this word. It is enjoined on the prayer of all "that it run its course"

(2 Th 3:1). The word spoken in the church is not merely the word of the apostles so that others would have only to listen to it, but it is the word of all who belong to the church. All have an ability and a right, indeed a duty, to speak the word: "When you come together, each has a psalm, a lesson, a revelation, a talking with tongues, an interpretation. Everything is to take place for edification" (1 Cor 14:26). This church, which has been aroused and set in motion in its totality by the word, is capable of winning over the unbeliever. Of this church Paul says: "When all are in the assembly proclaiming revelation* and an unbeliever or a non-initiate comes in, then he is convinced by all, judged by all. The secrets of his heart become manifest. He falls on his face, prays to God and confesses that God is really in your midst" (1 Cor 14:24f). Their testimony is to find expression at least in the Amen which the assembly speaks to the thanksgiving prayer of the prophet (1 Cor 14:16). In accord with this the writings of the New Testament inform us how in fact the whole apostolic church proclaimed the word. The Acts of the Apostles (4:31; see 8:4; 11:19) reports exultantly that "all filled with the spirit spoke the word of God with frankness." The church of Thessalonica made the word of the Lord resound in Macedonia and Achaea; indeed its belief had been noted everywhere (1 Th 1:8). While Paul is bound as a prisoner, the brothers proclaim the word in confidence (Phil 1:14). True,

* "Proclaiming revelation" (die Offenbarung verkünden) is a free adaptation of Paul's "prophesying" ($\pi\rho o\phi\eta\tau\epsilon\acute{v}\omega\sigma\iota\nu$) contrasted to "talking with tongues," in Paul's censure of overemphasis on that practice.

Paul cannot help hinting that it is only the majority of the brothers who are doing this, indeed that it is only recently that they are increasing their boldness—thus that they were afraid before. Still, his words testify only that the spirit even of the original apostolic church was burdened with human inadequacy. According to Heb 5:12, all in the church had to be "teachers." And granted that 1 Tim 2:12 bids the women listen and keep silent in the assembly, 1 Pt 3:1 enjoins on them a proclamation in keeping with their role, "to win without words."

The church is church of the word in an abundance of ways. It is church of the word for a profound reason: because in Christ its Lord the whole and definitive word of God has been spoken in the world (Heb 1:1), indeed because Christ is in person the word of God become man (Jn 1:14). Christ is the ratifying Amen of God (Ap 3:14). In Christ the whole Yes of God to the world has become manifest, that mighty, ratifying Yes which fulfills all God's promises to Jews and heathens and completes every begining. The apostles propagate this Yes in their preaching, and the church ratifies it to God's honor in the solemn Amen of its divine service (2 Cor 1:19f).

The word is poor in outward power, hence untainted with force. But it contains an abundance of the most precious goods: charity, truth, freedom, purity, joy, love, spirit. If this holds true of the human word, how much more of the word of God. If the church is formed by the word then it is filled with all these goods which are contained and come to pass in the advent of the word. May the wish of the apostle always be fulfilled in the church: "Let the word of

Christ dwell among you in its richness, in that you teach one another in all wisdom and give instruction in psalms, hymns, and spiritual canticles, in gratitude to God singing in your hearts"[6] (Col 3:16).

[6] It is well known that Evangelical theology takes special pains both with the exposition of the biblical word in individual instances and with the problem of the word in general (not always escaping the danger of declaring the word alone the basis and life of the church without fully appreciating the role of the sacraments).

If any proof should be needed that the ancient Catholic tradition knows the meaning of the word in the church and esteems it highly, then this is available in investigations such as those of Th. Soiron, *Heilige Theologie,* 1935; E. Eilers, *Gottes Wort,* 1941 (both books are on the theology of the word and of preaching according to St. Bonaventure); and R. Gögler, *Das Wesen des biblischen Wortes nach Origenes* (dissertation), 1953.

4 CULT

Wherever it may be, there will never be a religious communion without cult. The church too was from the outset a communion of cult. Everywhere cult exists when a community's communion with God is represented and brought to completion in word and act, experienced and made perceptible at least under the covering of symbol.

1. In Israel Jesus found the worship of God and the relation of the people to God already institutionalized in law and custom. He does not abolish these institutions; on the contrary, this cultic law is provided for in principle when he says that he has come not to abolish the law, but to fulfill it in accord with its true meaning. The progress of time was articulated and arranged by week, sabbath and feasts. Jesus does not do away with the sabbath. He only urges its true meaning, that is, that the sabbath is to be a day of rest and a blessing for men. Therefore one must be allowed to heal on the sabbath (Mk 3:4). Therefore the hungry disciples must be permitted to pluck ears of grain on the sabbath (Mk 2:27). According to the reports of all the gospels, Jesus also shared in celebrating the yearly feasts.

Jesus behaved similarly in regard to the offering of sacrifice. Here too he urges the true inward meaning. The God to whom man sacrifices is the Merciful. Therefore it is not possible to offer sacrifice and at the same time to violate the duties of love to one's neighbors (Mk 7:11). Sacrifice to God is possible and meaningful only when brotherly love is practiced at the same time with it. Whoever lives in conflict with his brother cannot live at peace with God (Mt 5:23f): "If you are bringing a gift to the altar and there recall that your brother has some complaint against you, then put your gift down near the altar, first leave the place and reconcile yourself with your brother. Then come and offer your gift." He acknowledges also the institution and commission of priesthood in Israel, when he says to the person he has healed: "Show yourself to the priests" (Mk 1:43). In the woe discourse against the Pharisees, his threat against insincere piety is united with a profound reverence for temple and cult: "The temple, which sanctifies the gold, is greater than the gold, and the altar, which sanctifies the gift-offering, is greater than the gift-offering. Whoever swears by the temple swears by him who dwells in it" (Mt 23:17f). According to Mt 17:24, Jesus also pays the temple tax. His purification of the temple of all mundaneness and irreverence reveals precisely his zeal for God's house. Zeal for the house of the Lord consumes him (Jn 2:17). Also his expression of sovereignty: "Here is more than the temple" (Mt 12:6), means not destruction, but a surpassing fulfillment of the old order. At Jesus' condemnation a part is played by the mysterious expression: "I shall demolish this temple made with hands and in three days build another not made with hands" (Mk 14:58). With this expression he is describing the new, eschatological community which he will build as a temple of God, thus essentially as a cultic community. (The restrictive application of this saying of the Lord to the resurrection alone is an interpretation of John's own— Jn 2:21—that comes into force when the original expression "another" is suppressed.) Finally, with profound meaning, Jesus, in the gospel narratives, understands and explains his death as a fulfillment of the ancient sacred ordinances of feast and sacrifice in Israel; he founds a new cultic rite in adapting the expression of Ex 24:8 to say that his blood creates a new covenant, just as Moses once sealed the covenant in the blood of a victim (Mk 14:24). The last evangelist perceives and testifies that the great cultic celebrations of the church have their basis in his death. The meaning of John's testimony (19:34) that blood and water flowed out of Jesus' side can hardly be other than that the sacraments of baptism and the Lord's supper have their foundation in Jesus' death on the cross.

Christ congratulates his disciples: "Blessed are your eyes in seeing and your ears in hearing" (Mt 13:16). He refers the captive John the Baptist to his deeds as well as to his preaching. Both identify him as Messiah (Lk 7:22). Christ sends his disciples out to preach and to heal (Lk 9:2). Their commission is word and deed. The apostles understand and discharge as their office the work of bringing "to the obedience of faith by word and work" (Rom 15:18). The communion of disciples takes its rise not only at hearing the message but also at beholding the work of healing. This beholding sees the individual deeds, but behind them sees the Son of God become man who does these works. Henceforth the source and fundament of the community of disciples will always be both hearing and beholding. As the proclamation is heard, so the cult is beheld. Therefore the church will be both church of the word and church of sacrament and cult. The incarnation which those first disciples experienced will, as long as salvation is entering into time and space, continue at once concealed and manifested in the covering of signs in which the priests discharge their sacramental action. But the holy activity practiced and institutionalized in the church initially arises and thereafter constantly issues from the action of its Lord and continues his saving work. The Christ of the Johannine farewell discourse (Jn 14:12) even promises the disciples that they will do mightier works than he. This can hold true only insofar as his working is limited by time and is ended in its visibility by his going away. Therefore it is as yet incomplete. As his work is preserved, continued and fulfilled in its meaning in the church, these works are mightier than the preceding. By virtue of the victory of their Lord the disciples complete the conquest of the world.

2. The original activity of Christ is the healing of the sick, which restores visibly the body, and deeper than this, the whole man.

That sicknesses and death exist in this world and time is, in the view of the New Testament, a sign that time and world are in trouble. In the beginning it was not so. For God, who is Salvation and Life, created the world in such a way that it was good. Therefore sickness and death in the world are something evil and against God; but in the under-

standing of the New Testament they are a sign that Satan
is wielding power in the world. Therefore Jesus can tell the
crippled woman whom he heals that Satan has bound her
eighteen years (Lk 13:10–17). As bringer of God's dominion, Christ joins battle with Satan by healings of the
sick, but especially, in the presentation of the New Testament, by expulsions of demons. There certainly existed
belief in demons over all the ancient world, in the Greco-
Roman as well as in the Jewish world of Jesus' time. In this
whole world magicians, prophets and priests take pains to
bring about the expulsion and banishment of demons. The
New Testament itself is aware that there is exorcism of
demons and healing of the possessed even outside the community of disciples (Mk 9:38–41; Acts 19:13–17). If the
New Testament shares this widespread belief, this means
that there is a genuine sense of darkness and of horror
which is justified. The New Testament leads this sense
deeper, to the insight that the horrible really does threaten
man: not merely evil as an idea, but evil as a living, effective
power that is directed to destroying man's life of body and
spirit. The New Testament certainly says that the mark of
this world is sin and decline. But it says all this with the
purpose of bringing its message—the good news that Jesus
has achieved victory over the Powers and that the believer
is sheltered by God's protection. Therefore when Christ
addresses the evil spirit in the sick man, he is standing at
the line of division between belief and unbelief. Where
God and the Adversary encounter each other, perhaps
everything can also be explained by natural causes. Nevertheless, when Jesus attacks Satan in the sick man, he knows

and says that everything created and natural is in jeopardy
of evil, but is also supported and sheltered in God's con-
tinuous creating. Christ invokes that creating as power of
healing against loss and death. When the dominion of God
breaks forth in Christ, it consists precisely in the healing of
distortion and destruction and in the restoration of order
and beauty, the wholeness and perfection of the original
creation. But the dominion of God is not yet complete with
that. The biblical miracle is the beginning of that completion which is imminent. It is a sign to man's deep and im-
passioned hope for God's saving work, a work here and now
already effective and destined someday to be completed.
It is no magic for the moment but is a breakthrough here
and now of God's dominion. Every single miracle is a
pledge and a part of the one mighty miracle, the entry of
God into the world for its release, its justification, its
reconciliation.

Out of the plenitude of his powers Jesus gives the disciples commission to heal the sick. The plain command:
"Heal the sick" (Mt 10:8)—received in faith—gives even
to them power over sickness. This power however was not
understood by them as a capacity for magic. They preserve
the saying of the Lord that only prayer can banish evil
(Mk 9:29). And the ability to heal is not the most important endowment of discipleship. Much more important
is election by the love of God: "Do not be joyful that
demons are subject to you. Rather be glad that your names
are written in heaven" (Lk 10:20). In the confidence of
belief the apostolic church undertook the healing even of
bodily infirmity and succeeded in it. This is what the Acts

of the Apostles reports (3:6f; 9:34; 16:18), as well as the concluding section of the Gospel of Mark, which dates from the late apostolic age (Mk 16:17f). According to Heb 2:4, God confirms the proclamation "by signs and miracles and manifold demonstrations of power and gifts of the Holy Spirit." Paul is certain that he has power to heal. In Rom 15:19 he declares that he possesses "the power of signs and miracles, the power of the spirit of God." He reminds the Corinthians (2 Cor 12:12) that as proof of his apostolic sending he exercised in their midst "perfect endurance, signs, miracles, deeds of power." Paul is just as certain that the power of healings has been given the church. In 1 Cor 12:9, 28, 30, he counts among the charisms "the charisms of healings"; in 1 Cor 12:10, "powers for deeds of might." But Paul too knows ways incomparably surpassing these: love (1 Cor 13) and the word of edification (1 Cor 14).

This, the church's gift of miracles, is certainly contingent on God's will. It is his to make this power become effective. Therefore the occurrence of sickness and death does not shock the faithful. The church cannot force and cannot extort the healings. It can only beg for an act of healing and must give thanks for it. The church's tradition knows that its very Savior could not heal everyone (Mk 1:34; 3:10). He was capable of healing only where he found belief (Mk 6:5f). Therefore Paul thanks God in prayer for the restoration to health of Epaphroditus, who has been sick to the point of death (Phil 2:26). In his own sickness he begs God for release (2 Cor 12:8). The church in Thessalonica must bear with the fact that believers die before the coming of

the Lord. Paul can do no more than offer them the consolation of faith (1 Th 4:18). The healing work of the church,
according to Jas 5:13–15, has been provided for in an
ecclesiastical institution. Granted, the church has uncon-
ditional and unrestricted assurance that its prayer "will
save the sick man, and the Lord will restore him." But the
healing is always God's gift. Here too then the intercession
of the presbyters, the "prayer of faith," is essentially important. If therefore, in accord with this ordinance, the
disciples of the Lord use a material substance—the oil—in
healing, whereas the Lord healed with his word alone, this
is an expression of fitting humility by which the church distinguishes itself from its Lord. But this way of proceeding
shows also that there is at work under the sign of the sacrament the healing hand and power of the Savior of the
church. The church has never forgotten the commission
of its Lord to heal the sick. Care for the sick has always
been dear to it. It established the first hospitals in the
world. In the mighty cities of antiquity which have been
reawakened from their ruins by excavations we find palaces
and cottages, temples and marketplaces, courts and theaters
and barracks, but no hospitals. St. Basil the Great, as
metropolitan of Caesarea, built and organized the first
hospital. Subsequently hospitals arose in every land. What
must seem to us a matter of obvious humaneness is often
enough a daughter of Christian *Caritas* who no longer
recognizes her mother. The church continues to carry out
its service to the sick. It is a daily task of the church's care
of souls.

3. Other activity of the church continues other work of
its Lord.

Its celebration of the meal makes present over and over again the manner in which Christ originally had united his group of disciples about him. After often holding fellowship at table with his men, and now while awaiting the time when mortal enmity would strike the shepherd, Jesus wanted to celebrate the meal a last time with them, in order once more to bring them all together with one another and with him as the center of their fellowship. If each meal united the group of disciples, then the fellowship of this last meal was of an altogether special profundity. Not only was it a festive Passover meal, the sort that created an intimate bond between the father of the household and his own.[1] This meal was a symbol of the imminent death of the Lord and, more, a foretaste of the future kingdom of God, which was represented here under the image of eschatological fellowship at table. All this is stated by the four reports of the last meal (Mk 14:12–25 with parallels, and 1 Cor 11:23–25).

In this last meal of Jesus with the disciples the cultic meal-celebration of the church was instituted. With Lk 22:19 and 1 Cor 11:25, the repetition of the meal takes place according to the express command of Jesus: "Do this in memory of me." In the reports of the Acts of the Apostles (2:46f), the primitive Jerusalem community celebrated this table fellowship not long after this. "They broke bread in the domestic communities, took food with joy and simplicity of heart, and praised God." The joy of the meal-celebration was certainly first of all joy in experiencing the

[1] The frequently discussed question of whether the last meal of Jesus was a Passover meal or not is answered convincingly in the affirmative by J. Jeremias in his careful study, *The Eucharistic Words of Jesus*, tr. A. Ehrhardt, New York 1960.

communion of the faithful; but then, deeper still, it was consciousness of communion with Christ, whom the community at supper believed and found present, just as he once had celebrated the meal with his own; and finally, it was exultation in looking forward to the approaching kingdom of God. In the sign of the broken bread and poured-out wine, the saving death of the Lord was both signified and present. By the explaining and accomplishing word, the Lord was made still more manifest and in sign and word thus "proclaimed until he should come again," as Paul expressed it (1 Cor 11:26). But death and resurrection, in which redemption had taken place, covered in their turn the return and the approach of the ultimate dominion of God. As expression of the community's assurance of communion with the Lord, the church prays at the supper the *Maranatha*, and Paul adopts this prayer (1 Cor 16:22).[2] And he goes on to say that the church is united in this meal as one body and formed into one body with the Lord. The sharing of the eucharistic bread is the sharing of the Lord's body. But the eucharistic body of the Lord then creates that other body which is the church: "We, that are many, are one bread and therefore one body" (1 Cor 10:16f).

The other main sign of salvation in the community of disciples is *baptism*. The sign content of an act of baptizing is evident: the outward washing in clean water is to image

[2] Paul clearly takes the prayer-invocation over from the divine service of the Palestine community. The invocation announces that the community united at divine service joins itself with its Lord—whether the invocation as used there means "our Lord is present" or "our Lord, come." See K. G. Kuhn in *Theologisches Wörterbuch zum Neuen Testament*, vol. 4, 470–475.

clearly the inward cleansing. It is not surprising that such a custom is practiced in many religions. The New Testament itself is aware that it has taken the custom over from John and thereby from Judaism. The consciousness of the most ancient tradition derives the church's practice of baptism from the commission of Jesus himself (Mt 28:19f; Jn 4:2). This tradition is thoroughly reliable because the church carried out baptism universally and with assurance from the very beginning. Whence does it have this assurance if not precisely from the command of its Lord? What baptism first works is forgiveness of sins, and with this the one baptized becomes a member of the messianic communion of the saints. The spirit which baptism bestowed meant that the end time had already begun, since the fulfillment of the spirit was expected precisely in the messianic age. Paul took over use and understanding of baptism from the primitive community, but he further developed and deepened its theology. In chapter 6 of his Letter to the Romans (similarly but more briefly in Col 2:12f), he expounds it: the descent into the baptismal bath and the reascent—Paul takes this ceremony as his point of departure—these signify death and resurrection with Christ. The one being baptized dies to the old life of sin and death and rises to the new life. The death and resurrection of the Lord are enacted in every believer through baptism. Risen in Christ, the Christian is another man, a new creation (2 Cor 5:17). But in the primitive community, as with Paul, baptism is not merely a symbol of this happening, but a creative and divine reality.

As a further activity carried out in cult, the New Testa-

ment names the *imposition of hands*. By this and the
simultaneous prayer of the apostles the Holy Spirit is
transmitted to the baptized (Acts 8:17–19; Heb 6:2). And
by prayer and imposition of hands power of office is transmitted to the apostles' assistants (Acts 6:6). When the
church of Antioch sends Barnabas and Paul out on mission,
it does so with an imposition of hands accompanied by
prayer and fasting (Acts 13:3). As early as the pastoral
letters it is an assured institution of the church that priests
are appointed through imposition of hands by apostles or
priests (1 Tim 4:14; 5:22; 2 Tim 1:6). The meaning of
the action is easy to recognize. The filled hand transfers to
the one it is laid on what belonged to the other. This
rite is performed both in extra-biblical religions and in the
Old Testament, whether it is to load guilt on a sacrificial
animal (Lv 16:21) or on a man (Lv 24:14), whether it is
to impart blessing (Gn 48:14) or to transfer spirit and
authority, as Moses transferred these gifts to Joshua by
imposition of hands (Nm 27:23; Dt 34:9). Jesus too
blesses the children by imposition of hands (Mk 10:16)
just as rabbis might do. In the time of the New Testament,
imposition of hands was the rite used in the rabbinate for
initiation into the office of teacher. If the imposition of
hands is performed in the church, it clearly occurs as adop-
tion of an ancient practice such as this. Imposition of hands
mediates spirit and authority and guarantees the uninter-
rupted apostolic succession.[3]

[3] The connections between the two traditions are comprehensively presented by E. Lohse, *Die Ordination im Spätjudentum
und im Neuen Testament*, 1951.

The divine life of the church has its source in cult. But then cult with its gifts and demands shapes also the church's daily *moral life*. The calling upon the Lord in community prayer must issue from a clean heart (2 Tim 2:22). Thus cult is a summons to an ever new cleansing. Baptism gives the believer confidence and joyfulness in faith since he knows that the heart as well as the body has been purified (Heb 10:22). But then baptism requires of the baptized in future a life free from sin, a life in truth and faith and in keeping with the spirit (Acts 2:38; Rom 6:12f; Heb 10:22; 1 Pt 3:21). Fellowship in the supper admonishes and obliges them both to keep far from strange gods and adhere to the Lord with whom the supper unites them inwardly, and to live in the communion of brotherly love and not destroy it by forming parties (1 Cor 10 and 11). The priest appointed by imposition of hands must understand and realize the gift transferred to him as a commission (2 Tim 1:6–9). And so cultic observance is thus the source and support of the existence and life of the church. The church is built up in the assembly of divine service (1 Cor 14:3–26).

4. In view of the importance which cult had for the New Testament church, it is not remarkable that the New Testament in numerous passages provides recognizable testimonies to the rituals of divine service. Testimonies to a cult already practiced occur as early as the stories which base the cultic observances of the church on the life of Jesus. In Mt 28:16–20, baptism is derived from a command of Jesus. The story already presumes the Christian practice of baptism and mirrors that practice. For in Mt 28:19f,

reception into the church is described as it takes place in the catechumenal process. First comes the exhortation to an instruction which precedes and prepares for the acceptance of faith ("Make them into disciples"); next follows the reception into the church by baptism in the name of the Trinity; and then the baptized is taught in particular about faith and life ("Teach them to observe all that I have commanded you"). The narratives of the supper also probably stem in the synoptic account (Mk 14:22–24) as in Paul (1 Cor 11:23–25) from the ritual of the church, in which the event of the supper in the past was narrated as a foundation document for the subsequent practice of the Lord's supper (just as it is to this day in the canon of the Mass). In this repetition of the story, the narrative gradually took on the ritual, stylized formulation, in which it meets us in the New Testament text. Within our fourfold tradition of the New Testament the ritual tone of the style appears to increase from the earlier to the later transmission.

We take also as testimonies to a cult already celebrated in the New Testament church those scriptural passages in which we can—with certainty or with probability— recognize confessional formulas, canticles and hymns of the primitive church. From earliest times onward the confession of faith held its place firmly in the divine service (1 Cor 12:3). The assembled church takes up the confession in ritual chorus as it answers with Amen (1 Cor 14:16; 2 Cor 1:20; Justin, *First Apology* 67). A confessional formula underlies 1 Cor 15:3f, in which the christological part of the Apostles' Creed, prayed to this day in the church, is already taking shape. In other places too we recognize the employment of the old christological confessional formulas, as in Peter's preaching of Acts 2:36; 3:13–15, and with Paul, for example, in Rom 10:6–9; Col 1:12–20.

The church composes canticles for divine service. Mary's canticle (Lk 1:46–55), Zachary's song of praise (Lk 1:68–79) and Simeon's canticle of thanksgiving (Lk 2:29–32)—all show that the church in keeping with Jewish tradition knows and creates hymns. Phil 2:5–11 is confession of faith and hymn to Christ in one. Careful exegesis has made it very highly probable that Paul is employing here a hymn which he finds ready at hand. No doubt one is right to conclude this from the unpauline language and perhaps even prepauline theology of the hymn.[4] But more, the very content of this hymn, in which Christ is confessed as *Kyrios* and all beings bow in homage before God and in honor of Christ, reflects what actually took place during the confession of faith in God and in the Lord at the divine service of the community. In 1 Tim 3:16 the incarnation and exaltation of the Redeemer are testified to in a rhythmically formed canticle. In Eph 5:14 an ancient baptismal canticle seems to have been retained. Form and thought obviously distinguish three canticles to Christ in 1 Pt 1:18–21; 2:21–25; 3:18–22. The canticles of praise in the Apocalypse (4:11; 5:9–13), which are directed to the enthroned God and the Lamb that was slain, had their

[4] These findings of the frequently cited, careful investigation of E. Lohmeyer, *Kyrios Jesus*, 1928, have met with widespread agreement.

counterparts in the ritualized liturgy of the church. Well-founded is the assumption that John the Evangelist (Jn 1:1–5, 9–14, 16–18) prefixes to his gospel a hymn to the Logos (found ready at hand as a cultic canticle of the community or perhaps earlier composed by himself).[5]

Paul presumes the celebration of divine service with canticle and confession of faith when he says that psalms are sung in divine service (1 Cor 14:26) and when he recommends the singing of inspired psalms, hymns and canticles (Col 3:16; Eph 5:19). But the magnificent liturgical images of the Apocalypse are surely formed by the visionary according to the celebrations which he himself had experienced and joined in celebrating at divine service in both synagogue and Christian gatherings.[6] At nearly the same time as the Apocalypse was written, Pliny the Younger (Letters 10:96–7) in his famous letter to the Emperor Trajan, says, as he describes the Christian divine service, that the Christians "assemble before sun-up on the established day to sing antiphonally a song to Christ as to a god." Thus from early times onward liturgical song was fostered in the divine service of the church.

5. We may still ask the question what function the apostles and superintendents of the church had in the cele-

[5] The reader might compare the commentaries on the Gospel of John by R. Bultmann, Theology of the New Testament, vols. 1, New York, 1953, 1–5, and by A. Wikenhauser, New Testament Introduction, New York 1963, 36f. See also R. Schnackenburg, "Logos-Hymnus und johanneischer Prolog," Biblische Zeitschrift, New Series, no. 1, 1956, 69–109.

[6] Exegesis raises the question whether John perhaps also made use of a knowledge of the gorgeous heathen cult; thus especially E. Stauffer, Christ and the Caesars, Westminster 1955.

bration of the divine service. Certainly the gatherings for divine service needed men to arrange and design them. But what sort of commission and significance did these arrangers have? Did they care only for outward, technical arrangements as, for example, prayer leaders and cantors do, or did they carry executive responsibility for the divine service as do priests?

In regard to baptism our accounts say clearly enough that the apostles themselves baptized or left baptizing to others. Paul expressly says (1 Cor 1:14–17) that his mission is preaching, not baptizing. It would be altogether erroneous to gather from this that Paul esteemed the sacrament less in comparison with the word. No one can value the sacrament more highly than Paul does in Rom 6 and 1 Cor 10 and 11. The conferring of the sacrament is not a lesser but rather another task than that of the apostle. It may be that Paul already knows the arrangement of baptism into catechumenal process, solemn rite of conferring, and subsequent further instruction. But the onward-driving missionary must leave the practice of this institution to others, even though his preaching has no other goal than to lead to the sacrament. Imposition of hands is discharged, according to the New Testament, by those who are themselves endowed with the spirit or are holders of office: according to Acts 6:6; 8:17–19; 1 Tim 4:14; 5:22; according to 2 Tim 1:6, by the apostles; but according to Acts 13:3, probably also by the prophets and teachers along with the whole church of Antioch. In the description of how the sacrament of healing the sick is discharged (Jas 5:14f), it is presumed that the presbyters as a special class in the church perform the ceremony. They must be called to it, because it is only they who are authorized and qualified for it. The word "presbyter" (that is, "elder") does not require that those who perform the rite be the oldest in the community according to actual age, but the word is assuredly a title and class designation (see 136f). And what was the arrangement at the Lord's supper? According to Acts 20:7–11, Paul preached at the celebration of the breaking of bread in the community at Troas and himself performed the breaking of bread. There would naturally have been such deference to the preeminent authority of the apostles that wherever an apostle was present it was he who celebrated the liturgy of the supper with word and action: on such occasions, then, as immediate witness of the life of Jesus, he repeated the account of the celebration of the meal by Jesus himself and thereby renewed it. The office of apostle naturally attracted the function of divine service to itself. When, according to Acts 6:4, the apostles "persevere in prayer and in the ministry of the word," this means not a private—or certainly not only a private—but above all a public and liturgical prayer. But then how was it when no apostle was present? Then the superintendents of the community would have taken over their places, just as Paul commissioned them to do in the communities which had achieved at least a certain independence. Timothy, a superintendent of this sort, is admonished: "Until I return, continue to read the lessons, to exhort, and to teach" (1 Tim 4:13). If reading the lessons takes place in the divine service, so, probably, does exhortation and teaching. Timothy is thus leader of the assembly at

divine service. But how was the service previously con-
ducted, especially in those places where not even appointed
community leaders such as these were available? Had superintendents such as these, empowered for the liturgy,
already been appointed at Corinth so that they thus would
have celebrated the Lord's supper, as 1 Cor 10 and 11 show?
How was it in the domestic communities at Jerusalem (Acts
2:46)? The New Testament and, near to the New Testament in time, the *Didache* probably give us an answer to
such questions. According to Acts 13:1f, prophets and
teachers in the church of Antioch celebrate "the liturgy to
the Lord." The *Didache* prescribes: "Let the prophets
celebrate the Eucharist as often as they want" (10:7).
"Eucharist" here will mean not merely the prayer of thanksgiving after the Lord's supper, but the whole "eucharistic
supper-ritual." The prophets thus have a priestly function,
just as the *Didache* 13:7 says of them: "The prophets are
your high priests." According to this, the prophets, as
charismatic office holders immediately appointed by God,
celebrated the liturgy and the Eucharist. It may hold true
even for the New Testament time that not only apostles
and the overseers commissioned by them, but also persons
with charismatic vocations such as the New Testament
prophets (Eph 2:20) carried out priestly ministry.[7]

The definitive institution which sets off the ordained
priest with his cultic-sacramental task from the "laymen"
is clearly attested at the turn of the first century. In the
First Letter of Clement (40:5) it is recalled that high-

---

[7] See on this point O. Casel, "Prophetie und Eucharistie,"
Jahrbuch für Liturgiewissenschaft 9, 1929, 1–19.

priests, priests and levites always have special roles to fulfill in the ministry of cult. Adding to this, the author admonishes that everybody in the church too should observe "the fixed institution of his cultic ministry in dignity (1 Clem 41:1). And Ignatius provides that "no one do anything in the church without the bishop. Let no Eucharist be held legitimate unless it is discharged with the bishop presiding or some one commissioned by him. . . . Without the bishop no one is privileged either to baptize or to celebrate the Agape" (To the Smyrneans 8:1f). We have every right to say that an institution which was provided and established as early as the New Testament has here found its authentic conclusion.

Church cult takes place principally in the discharge of sacramental procedures and transactions. But not only in these. The proclamation and hearing of the word in the assembled community also has cultic form, just as the response of the community to the word, the thanksgiving for the revelation, and the confession of the proclaimed word is cult whenever "in Christ the Amen of the church resounds to God" (2 Cor 1:20).

When 1 Jn 5:5–8 names "the three that give testimony" as "spirit, water, and blood," the apostle's meaning is probably first the baptism and death of Christ as beginning and completion of his work, then also the baptism which Christ has left to the church and the meal in which the cup with his blood maintains the new covenant—both sacraments being efficacious as powers of the spirit. The church's three mighty realities of salvation are thus baptism, the body and blood of the Lord that are present in the meal,

and the spirit of the transfigured Christ. The church receives these gifts in cultic celebration. Therefore Heb
10:25 admonishes: "We want our assemblies not to be
neglectful, as many often are, but rather to encourage one
another all the more." The letter is acquainted with the
meaning of the divine ministry and the cultic celebration
for the church. Subsequent writings from the times of the
early church continue such admonitions (see *Didache* 4:2,
16:2; Ignatius, *To the Trallians* 12:2; *To the Ephesians* 13;
Barnabas 4:10). From primitive church tradition, Ignatius
describes the meaning and power of the cult: "Be eager
frequently to come together for the Eucharist of God and
for praisegiving. For when you come together frequently,
the powers of Satan are brought to nothing, and his power
to corrupt is destroyed in the unity of your faith" (*To the
Ephesians* 13:1). But the Apostles' Creed comprehends the
church above all as *communio sanctorum*, that is, as communion (or fellowship) in the Holy, as communion which
is begun and maintained by the sacraments.[8]

---

[8] In the formula "*communio sanctorum*," "*sanctorum*" is originally understood as the genitive, not of *sancti* (holy persons), but of
sancta (holy things). See the clarification of this meaning and a
comprehensive presentation of the history of the formula's signification in J. R. Geiselman, *Die theologische Anthropologie Johann
Adam Möhlers*, 1955, 56–106.

5 THE APOSTLE AS PRIEST

"TO BE A PRIEST OF THE GOSPEL"
(ROMANS 15:16)

Protestant exegesis and theology understand the apostolic office almost exclusively as ministry of the word. Only the church as a *whole* would be conscious of holding commission for priestly ministry. The New Testament would not recognize the priesthood of individual office holders. As the judgment of an undisputed representative of Protestant New Testament theology one might cite the saying of R. Bultmann: "The community has no need of persons of special quality, that is, of priests, to mediate between the community and God" (*Theologie des Neuen Testaments*, 3rd. ed., 1958, 117; see 153f, 461f). In contrast to this, our question will be whether and how a priestly service of the apostolic office is announced and given its foundation in the New Testament.[1]

---

[1] As more recent works on the question, the following should be named: H. Asmussen, *Das Priestertum aller Gläubigen*, 1947; H. von. Campenhausen, *Kirchliches Amt und geistliche Vollmacht*, 1953; W. Michaelis, *Das Ältestenamt der christichen Gemeinde im Lichte der Heiligen Schrift*, 1953; E. Schweizer, *Church Order in the New Testament*, Naperville 1961; O. Semmelroth, *Das geistliche Amt*, 1958; C. Spicq, *La Spiritualité sacerdotale d'après saint Paul*, 1954; E. Walter, "Diener des Neuen Bundes," *Quellen*

1. What is the essence of the priesthood according to the New Testament? We can obtain an answer to this question from 1 Pt 2:1–9.[2] Certainly the passage deals not with the special and individual priesthood, but with the general priesthood of the church. Yet at the same time it says what constitutes the priesthood. It indicates a double commission and service as essential to priesthood: testimony and sacrifice, or, expressed more generally, word and cult.

One of the elements, one that belongs in essence to the priesthood, is named by 1 Pt 2:9: "But you are a select generation, a royal priesthood, a holy class, a people appointed to be his own, that you may proclaim the mighty deeds of him who has called you from the darkness into his wonderful light. Once you were a people that did not exist, but now you are God's people; once you were left without mercy, but now you are taken up in mercy." The word of testimony is thus the first element that constitutes the priesthood. Certainly much is said among men about God. But this word of priestly ministry is a special word, other than that which the history of religion or philosophy may say about God. It does not speak of the idea of God, of God in himself, but of God who has dealt and still deals in history and world with mighty deeds of salvation. These

---

lebendigen Wassers, 1953, 223–270; K. Weiss, "Paulus, Priester der Kultgemeinde," Theologische Literaturzeitung 79, 1954, col. 355–364. The English reader is also referred to Bultmann's two-volume Theology of the New Testament, New York, a translation of the above-quoted work.

[2] For an exposition of 1 Pt 2:5, 9, see finally J. Blinzler, "Hierateuma," Episcopus, Festschrift für Kardinal Faulhaber, 1949, 49–65.

deeds have taken place for faith and in the community of the church and have been concealed from the world. But God's priestly people has to testify to these deeds and proclaim them in public to the world. The passage might suggest to us that what also distinguishes this proclamation from a merely human religious word that it is made in virtue of the God who reveals himself in it. For the God whose mercy and power have summoned from the darkness into light thereafter accompanies those to whom he has given vocation and grace—accompanies them, and speaks in them, by them, from them.

The other essential task of the priesthood is sacrifice: "Let yourselves be built up as living stones into a temple in the Holy Spirit, into a holy priesthood, to present sacrifices in which the spirit works and which are well pleasing to God through Jesus Christ" (1 Pt 2:5). The letter knows that no man can offer sacrifice to God simply on his own initiative so that the sacrifices would have meaning and value. They are possible in the church only through their being presented and celebrated by Christ, thus in communion with him who is the one Priest of the church. And they continue to be possible only if the spirit of God is at work in these sacrifices and dominates them throughout; they are possible only as sacrifices worked by the spirit. Thus it is also said here that New Testament priesthood can never come forward and work on its own initiative. It is possible and actual only as a share in the priesthood of Christ and as a ministry in the spirit at work in the church.

But both tasks of priestly ministry, word and cult, have

a common note, namely the function of mediation. The word mediates insofar as it reveals the hidden works of God to the world. The word is mediative also because in it the power of God testifies to itself in the world. But also clearly mediative is the other priestly service, sacrifice, which is always a transaction between earth and heaven. Thus the ministry of mediation in word is a transaction from God to the world, that of sacrifice—however, one from the world to God. Priesthood certainly stays in the world; yet it is set apart from the world, in that it stands between God and the world. This setting-apart is also expressed in the accompanying words with which Peter characterizes priesthood. He calls it "holy, select, called, taken up in mercy." It is well known that "holy" is not originally an ethical term. According to the Old and New Testaments, God is the original Holy One, the qadosh, that is (in the original signification of the word), one who is "separated," separated from the condition of a creature and beyond the world, the "wholly other." And the holy are those who are drawn out by him from the world and belong to him— the angels, the church. Then the further expressions, "select," "called," "taken up in mercy," are thus only the unfolding of the first expression, "holiness." All these expressions are such that they ascribe to those characterized by them not merely a task which one does once and then steps back from, but a permanent staying and abiding in a task, in a service, in a distinct and separate class.

That we have rightly ascertained here the notion and content of priesthood is confirmed for us when we establish that the Old Testament priesthood had the same commissions. According to Dt 33:8–11, the Old Testament priesthood has the service of divination by lots, of instructing in the law, and of sacrifice. Thus it too is word and cult. The word is also mediative insofar as it makes known to his people the will of God in the Law; that the sacrifice is a ministry of mediation needs no demonstration. The same thing presents itself to us, according to the New Testament, as the essential commission of the Jewish highpriest. His duties of office are above all those of cult. But he has also to mediate God's word to the people. Therefore, according to Jn 11:51, the highpriest is capable of the prophetic pronouncement that Jesus will perish for the people and for the world.[3] In the community of Qumran the priests have the task of teaching as well as the task of presiding over the cultic action. Thus they lead the celebration of the meal and the divine service just as they preside authoritatively over the exposition of scripture.

2. Let us listen to the testimony of the New Testament on how the mediative-priestly ministry of word and cult is discharged in the office of apostle. The question will be put first with regard to the creation of the apostolate according to the gospels, then with regard to the exercise of the apostolate in the church according to the Acts of the Apostles and the letters of the apostles.

In the story of the vocation of the disciples (Mk 1:16–20) stands the vocation-giving expression of Jesus: "Follow me, and I shall make you fishers of men." Those called

[3] The history and phenomenology of religions continue to confirm that the priesthood everywhere has the double service named above as its essential tasks. The reader might confer G. van der Leeuw, *Phänomenologie der Religion*, 2nd ed., 1956, 240–243.

were taking fish from the sea before this; in future they will take men. Just as the fish were in the sea, men are in the world. On the shore of the sea of the world stand the disciples. They gather men from the world. What for? In the language of the synoptics, for entering into the royal dominion of God. Thus the disciples stand in a mysterious center—between the world and the royal dominion of God, between the past and the future, between men and God. They have been drawn out from the world and stand as ministers of the Lord who calls them and as ministers in the name of God. To this end they are created anew. "He saw them . . . and called them . . . : I shall make you fishers of men."

The passage thus contains this essential assertion on the office of the apostles: they have been called to a ministry of mediation between God and men and to this end have been created anew.

Then the disciples are sent out as the twelve apostles. In this instance Mk 3:14f says: "He created the Twelve, that they might be with him and that he might send them out to preach and have power to expel evil spirits."[4]

The apostolic service has been described as a double one: as commission to proclaim and commission to heal, as word and work. But such is also precisely the service of the Lord himself. In both ways he brings and effects God's royal dominion among us. As his word announces the royal dominion, that royal dominion comes on the scene (Lk 4:18–21). Of his work of salvation he himself says that God's royal dominion has indeed come when he expels

[4] For a further explanation of Mk 1:16–20, see above, 9–15.

demons by the finger of God (Lk 11:20). If he effects God's dominion by word and work, then the disciples are to do it in the same way. Thus it becomes clear how their service is mediative precisely between God's royal dominion and the world. But the very identity between Jesus' messianic ministry and their apostolic ministry makes it manifest that the apostle stands as a minister of the Messiah, indeed continues the Messiah's own ministry and carries it out. His ministry is thus never autonomous and independent, but a share and a part of the ministry of Christ. This was also implied when it was declared of the apostle that he was to stay with the Lord and was to be sent out (Mk 3:14). Even when sent out as messenger, the apostle stays united with the Lord. This unity between the one sending and the one sent out is then expressly declared in the principle: "Whoever receives you receives me, and whoever receives me receives him who has sent me" (Mt 10: 40). And again, Lk 10:16: "Whoever hears you hears me, and whoever despises you despises me, and whoever despises me despises him who has sent me." Similarly Jn 13:20; 17:18. When Peter is commissioned: "Pasture my lambs" (Jn 21:15, 17), he is in fact *vicarius Christi*: it is Christ who is the real shepherd of the church. So the service of the apostles appears once again in a new aspect as mediative: they mediate to the world the messianic salvation of their Lord who sends them out, and in doing so they mediate the salvation of the eternal God.

That the word of the apostles is more than mere communicating and reporting, that it is rather a mediation of God's salvation, in that the word of God arriving in the

word of the apostles brings with it God's gift of salvation—
we have already shown this in our examination of the New
Testament.[5] But if the word of the church should ever come
to exercise a teaching or disciplinary force (this is what
the saying of Mt 16:19 and 18:18 means: "Whatever you
will bind on earth . . . , whatever you will loose on earth,
will be bound and loosed in heaven too"), then these
earthly decisions hold true in heaven. "God's judgment is
not merely proclaimed in the church, but carried out. The
church's conduct of affairs is the present conduct of affairs
of God himself."[6] This is precisely the declaration of Jn
20:22f: "Receive the Holy Spirit. Whomever you release
from his sins, he is released from them. Whomever you
hold to them, he is held to them." Forgiveness of sins is
thus the fully decisive gift which the disciples have to with-
hold from or mediate to the world. This capacity they have
from the spirit that testifies efficaciously in them of Jesus
(Jn 15:26: "The spirit of truth that proceeds from the
Father will give testimony of me"). This spirit convicts the
world of sin (Jn 16:8: "He will come and will convict the
world of sin, of justice, and of judgment"). But the spirit
also creates the world anew (Jn 3:5f: "Whoever has not
been born anew of water and spirit cannot enter the royal
dominion of God") and makes it living (Jn 6:63: "It is
the spirit that makes live; the flesh avails nothing"). The

[5] See above, 61–64.
[6] This is how H. von Campenhausen, op. cit. 137–143, interprets Mt 16:19 and 18:18. True, he means that there is no question
of genuine sayings of Jesus here, but of later constructions of the
church, since the church's existence is already presumed in both
sayings.

mercy and the salutary will of the eternal Father work on the world in the office of the apostles (Jn 20:21: "As the Father has sent me, so I send you").

Jesus never speaks expressly of a priestly commission of his disciples and apostles. But the apostolic ministry is instituted by the word of the Lord of the church, and it is instituted here as mediative and thereby as a real priestly ministry.

If we turn to the other question, whether and how the church of the apostles understood and exercised the apostolic office as priestly, then we must certainly confirm that the writings of the New Testament nowhere speak expressly and with the usual word ἱερεύς of priests among the holders of office. Yet the apostles exercise a ministry of mediation in word and action, and at any rate Paul has profoundly understood his ministry as a priestly ministry.

The apostles carry out such ministry, according to the Acts of the Apostles, when (Acts 1:8) the power of the Holy Spirit expresses itself in their testimony ("You will receive the power of the Holy Spirit, who is coming down on you, and be witnesses to me to the ends of the earth"), or again when (Acts 8:15–18) the newly baptized in Samaria receive the spirit through imposition of hands by Peter and John (the apostles are thus mediating tools of the spirit); further when (Acts 15:28) the Spirit speaks in the word of the apostles ("It has pleased the Holy Spirit and us") and when (Acts 20:28) the Holy Spirit appoints the bishops and presbyters, an event that certainly took place by human mediation. The simple conjunction in this passage of Holy Spirit and apostles, as also in Acts 15:28, suffices to span the mystery of the with-each-other and in-each-other of God and church, of eternal and temporal.

When the preaching is as it should be, it is the spirit that produces the effect (1 Pt 1:12: "The proclamation took place through those who brought you the glad tidings in the power of the Holy Spirit sent from heaven"), just as it is the spirit who gives to the church the word as weapon in battle (Eph 6:17: "Grip the sword of the spirit, which is the word of God"). In the institution of the anointing of the sick (Jas 5:14f: "If anyone among you is sick, then let him call to him the presbyters of the church. They are to pray over him and anoint him with oil in the name of the Lord. The prayer of faith will save the sick one, and the Lord will lift him up. If he has committed sins, they will be forgiven him"), it is not some sort of charismatic endowment that manages to heal, but a class, the class of presbyters. The power to heal is thus united with the office and, to be sure, permanently united with it. But the effects of prayer and of sacred actions are such that they can come only from God. Thus God's gift of healing is mediated by the person and the office of the presbyters.

Paul himself attests to us his knowledge of his priestly ministry. He knows himself commissioned to a ministry of the word. In this ministry, his speech is not just a teaching that stems from what a man knows and from a vocation he has taken on himself: it is God who speaks in his word. According to Eph 3:2–5 ("By revelation the mystery has been made known to me . . . as it is known by revelation to his holy apostles and prophets"), special insight into the mystery of Christ has been imparted to the apostle.

Apostles and prophets are bearers of the revelation of God. Paul has to mediate the revelation to the church by his proclamation. In this the apostles and prophets are designated even as *holy* apostles and prophets. If, assuredly, the whole church is holy, then these have been singled out as a special sanctified class of the church and stand apart in it.

This is why Paul can say of his word that he does not speak with any claim of his own, but with the power of the grace that has been given him (Rom 12:3: "I command you by the grace of the office that has been given me"), and can say that God's spirit and power are at work in his word (1 Cor 2:4: "My speech and my preaching did not consist in persuasive words of wisdom, but in the proof of spirit and power"). He is willing to deliver to the Corinthians at their request proof that Christ speaks in him (2 Cor 13:3: "You look for proof that Christ speaks in me. . . . He will not be weak in your regard, but powerful"). To the church in Thessalonica Paul writes that his gospel comes to them "not just in word, but also in power and in the Holy Spirit and in full confidence" (1 Th 1:5). Indeed Paul is capable of saying directly that the word of human preaching is God's word: "You have not accepted the word of God's preaching coming from us as word of man, but as what it is in reality, God's word which even now is at work among you the faithful" (1 Th 2:13). But to the church in Corinth Paul says that the word of reconciliation has been given in commission to the apostles— not only in such a way that they are to report about the reconciliation which took place at one time once and for all

in the cross of Christ, but in such a way that the reconciliation of the world is worked here and now by the apostolic
word of reconciliation: "He gave us the office of reconciliation, because God indeed was in Christ, reconciled the
world to himself, and established the word of reconciliation among us" (2 Cor 5:18–20). God's action in Christ
thus comprehends both, both the reconciliation itself and
the promulgation of the word of reconciliation. In the word
the reconciliation of God continues here and now to be
worked. Thus it is always coming anew into effect and com-
pleting itself. Therefore Paul says at last that the word
of the apostle is like the very word of Christ: "In Christ's
place we exercise office, as if God admonished through us.
We beseech you in place of Christ, let yourselves be reconciled with God."

Thus if the ministry of the apostle is capable of causing
reconciliation with God, then it is also capable of consign-
ing to the opposite of reconciliation, that is, rejection by
God. In 1 Cor 5:3–5, Paul performs an act of church
discipline. The community assembles in the spirit of Jesus;
Paul is with them, present in spirit, and in the power of the
Lord gives the sinner over to Satan for perdition of his
flesh, that his spirit may be saved on the day of the Lord.
Certainly the apostle joins with the church in doing this,
and he knows that he cannot perform an act which reaches
from earth into another world by his own power, but only
by the power of the Lord. Yet it is *he* who speaks and deals
decisively. It is *he* who gives the sinner over to Satan for
ruin of the flesh. There is no question in the apostle's mind
that the judgment will be effective and will take place.

Precisely in this way the apostle executes a penitential judgment which reaches into the world beyond. He gives Hymenaeus and Alexander over "to Satan, that they may be disciplined" (1 Tim 1:20). The apostle has in the church not only the right to advise, to admonish, to bid. He judges, and therein his judgment on the corporal, spiritual and eternal life of the faithful is decisive.

That the fate of the world is decided at the apostle's word, that judgment takes effect at his instance is finally also what the metaphor of 2 Cor 2:14–16 means: "By us God everywhere diffuses the fragrance of his knowledge. For we are the good odor of Christ unto God among the saved as well as among the lost—to the latter a scent of death bringing to death, to the former a fragrance of life bringing to life." The image used by Paul should be interpreted in light of the ancient notion which considered a fragrance something substantial on which plants, beasts and men can live or from which they must die if it is poisonous. Also applicable is another notion, that revelation of the divinity is accompanied by a good odor.[7]

According to this passage, Paul says that when God is known a fragrance giving power and life pours out on the world. First it quickens and fills the apostle with life by

[7] Thus Jb 14:9 is testimony to the belief that a tree reduced to a stump receives power to renew its life from the scent of water. Aristotle certainly disputes, yet mentions the assumption of the Pythagoreans "that many living beings take nourishment from scent." See the instances of this notion with C. Delling in *Theologisches Wörterbuch zum Neuen Testament*, vol. 5, 492–495; and E. Lohmeyer, *Vom göttlichen Wohlgeruch*, 1919.

making him into the good odor of Christ. The apostle will spread this fragrance with powerful effect. But thereupon the aptitude of man for life or for death becomes manifest through the apostle's office and through his own person. From other expressions of Paul we shall understand him here to the effect that those who experience the fragrance leading to life experience this according to God's choice, and those who experience the scent leading to death are already in death. But it is Paul's apostolic ministry which manifests the division, indeed causes it. Thus the apostolic ministry mediates the quickening power of God to the world, and by it the division and decision between death and life takes place.

Paul expresses still more clearly his possession of mediative-priestly commission in the world and over the world. The most penetrating expression is that of Rom 15:15–19: "The merciful commission of God has been given me, to be a *liturgos* for Christ Jesus unto the heathen, one who discharges the gospel of God in sacred ministry, that the heathen may become a sacrificial gift well-pleasing to God, sanctified in the Holy Spirit. . . . Christ worked through me to produce the heathens' obedience of faith through my word and work."* What an awareness the apostle possesses

---

* Λειτουργός with its cognates usually designates one who is responsible for or performs or leads some public service, a magistrate or public minister, sometimes a leader of public worship. The term therefore can be suggestive of a priestly function. More suggestive is the phrase "who discharges . . . in sacred service" (ἱερουργοῦντα: "to be a priest" in the title of this chapter). This expression has even etymological affinity with the usual word for priest ἱερεύς), though, as the author says, priesthood is not expressly counted among the New Testament offices.

here! His expression is full of intensive cultic terminology. He stands in the world as *liturgos*. His service is that of preparing the heathen to be a holy sacrificial gift. According to his expression, he carries out this service "by word and work." Both belong together not by way of addition, but in an indivisible unity. The work takes place in the word, and the work takes place in accord with the effective word. Thus it is his commission to carry out the consecration of the world. He is a priest who brings the world as sacrifice to God. He is not capable of this by his own power, but only God's spirit itself is capable of sanctifying and consecrating this sacrifice. Yet it is through Paul's ministry that it all takes place.

This testimony of Paul is not altogether the only instance in his letters; it is confirmed by other, sometimes merely allusive expressions. According to Rom 1:9f, Paul discharges his office as a sacred cult: "God, before whom I carry out sacred ministry in preaching the gospel of his Son—he is my witness how I remember you without ceasing by my prayers." In proclamation as in prayer Paul discharges his sacred ministry and acts as priest. Again, he understands his work of mission not merely as teaching, but as work of cult. And Paul writes the Philippians from captivity: "If I too am poured out as a sacrifice in the sacrifice and liturgy of your faith, then I am glad" (2:17). The church of Philippi celebrates the sacrifice and the divine service of faith. But the community certainly cannot step before God without a priest, no more so now than on the day of the Lord's coming (thus, Phil 2:16: "You are

my boast on the day of Christ").* Thus Paul is united
with his beloved community as its priest. With the sacrific-
ing community he steps before God as priest of the sacrificial action and at the same time as sacrificial gift whose
offering up accompanies this sacrifice. If, as he faces death,
the apostle finally says that his blood is being poured out
like a libation, then we shall understand him to mean that
he recognizes his whole life as a sacrifice: "I am already
on the point of being sacrificed.* The time of my departure
is at hand" (2 Tim 4:6).

Paul goes on to say of his suffering and dying that it works
life and salvation for the church (2 Cor 1:6: "If we are in
distress, this takes place for your consolation and your
salvation"; 2 Cor 4:12: "Thus death is at work in us, but
in you life"). Yet we may not explain even this claim
merely on the ground that late Judaism knew something of
the vicarious worth of innocent suffering.[8] Does Paul not
say this too from the consciousness of his priestly service?

* The passage alluded to stresses Paul's reliance on his charges'
giving a good account of themselves rather than their reliance on
his prayer and sacrifice. The element focused on in the author's
use of the passage is the closeness of the bond which exists between
Paul and his charges. Indeed this reciprocal concern is the burden
of the whole passage, even of those parts quoted just previously by
the author.

* "Sacrificed," or "poured out as a libation" ($\sigma\pi\acute{\epsilon}\nu\delta o\mu\alpha\iota$: the
Vulgate delibor).

[8] Often expressions are cited such as that of 4 Mac 17:22, written
probably in apostolic times: "Yet the martyrs have become as it
were a ransom for the sins of the people. By the blood of the pious
and their expiating death, divine providence has saved Israel sorely
distressed until now." See E. Lohse, Martyrer und Gottesknecht,
1955, 64–110.

He uses the image and language of sacrifice in 2 Cor 12:15:
"I will gladly offer up, yes be entirely offered up, for your
souls." In vicarious suffering even to sacrifice, Paul wants
to have been offered up for the church. Colossians 1:24
shows a way into the mysterious depths of serving and self-
offering for others: "I am filling up the measure of Christ's
affliction in my life for his body, which is the church." In
the continuation of the passion of its Lord, the church, as
the other body of Christ, has to endure and fulfill even to
eschatological completeness a fixed measure of suffering.
Paul exults that he shares in filling up this measure by all
his distresses and thus shares in bringing closer the day of
eschatological fulfillment for the church.

The apostle mediates God's work of salvation to the
world. This holds so utterly true that the New Testament
is capable of naming the apostles co-workers of God. As
early as Mt 9:37f, they are designated as workers in God's
harvest ("Bid the Lord of the harvest send workers into
his vineyard"). The harvest, the eschatological harvest of the
world, is God's harvest. He himself brings it in. But the
apostles help God so that the great harvest is brought in.
Then the apostles are designated by Paul even as co-workers
of God, as συνεργοὶ θεοῦ (1 Cor 3:9: "We are God's co-
workers, but you are God's arable land, God's building"; 1
Th 3:2: "Timothy, our brother and God's co-worker").
Now this is certainly such an exalted assertion that in
ancient and modern times it has been doubted whether
Paul really intends and says this. When Paul speaks of
συνεργοί in other passages, he means *his* co-workers, men who
work together *with him*. For this reason, exegesis asks

whether 1 Cor 3:9 too is to be so taken that Paul wants
to say: we the apostles are workers with one another in the
service of God. Yet careful attention to the language of
Paul makes it very probable that he is in fact designating
himself and the other apostles as God's co-workers.[9] This
interpretation is supported in the other passage, 1 Th 3:2.
To be sure, only part of the manuscripts read here συνεργὸν
τοῦ θεοῦ, the others διάκονον τοῦ θεοῦ or similarly.* All the
same, the textual critics and editors today mainly favor the
text συνεργὸν τοῦ θεοῦ, because it is only from this reading that
the different transmitted texts can be explained. To the
question that immediately must be put, the question why
the ancient transmission changed the word συνεργός into
διάκονος, our editors answer that apparently the former expression seemed too exalted. It is in fact an extraordinary
expression to say that the apostle is God's co-worker. Thus
God and his apostle work on the same level at one identical
work. God is active through the apostles, he works his salvation on the world through the apostles. Indeed both work
hand in hand. If this holds true in the objective order, still
it is true, even in human understanding, that the work of
man is meaningless in comparison with God's gift—just as
Paul earlier had occasion to say: "I planted, Apollos wa-
tered, but God gave the growth. Thus neither the one who

[9] The genitive with συνεργός always indicates the one who is the
opposite partner in the work. Then in 1 Cor 3:9 God is the one
whom the apostle works along with. The explanations of the com-
mentators and lexicons are divided between the two syntactically
possible interpretations named above.

* E.g., καὶ συνεργόν / καὶ διάκονον τοῦ θεοῦ / καὶ διάκονον τοῦ θεοῦ
καὶ συνεργὸν ἡμῶν / διάκονον καὶ συνεργὸν τοῦ θεοῦ.

plants nor the one who waters is anything, but the one who gives the growth, God" (1 Cor 3:6f).

If with all this we understand the apostolic ministry rightly from Paul's grasp of it, then we may also perhaps explain in accord with it two expressions in the Second Letter to the Corinthians which a reader will no doubt usually pass over. It may not be accidental that they stand in the same letter in which Paul testifies to the magnitude of the apostolic service as he does nowhere else.

One expression is that of 2 Cor 1:15. Paul is speaking of his traveling plans. He had by then long wanted to come back to Corinth "ἵνα δευτέραν χάριν σχῆτε" (that you might have the second charis). What does χάριν say here? Does it mean the friendly favor of Paul, as if to say that Paul wanted by his visit to give a new demonstration of his amiability and concern? But χάρις elsewhere in Paul never means human favor, but always divine grace. Thus he is saying here that the apostle's visit is a mediation of divine grace-giving in his community. Salvation comes with the office, indeed with the person of the apostle.[10]

The other expression is that of 2 Cor 8:23. Here Paul terms certain co-workers (not mentioned by name) ἀπόστολοι ἐκκλησιῶν, δόξα χριστοῦ. One can often read the translation: the apostles are the praise and honor of Christ, that is, praise and honor for Christ. However there is scarcely a

[10] Then we shall have to understand also Rom 1:10–15 in precisely the same way. Paul wants to see the community in Rome that he may "strengthen them with spiritual gifts of grace." And he comes, according to Rom 15:29, "with the plenitude of Christ's blessing." His office and his person, which bears the office, convey grace and blessing.

single instance in the New Testament when δόξα means
honor; rather, in accord with the use of the word in the
Greek Old Testament, it almost always means *revelation
of the glory of God*. Paul uses this word very frequently,
indeed in the same letter (2 Cor 3, 4), to indicate the
glory of God revealing itself in the apostolic office. Then
is it not likely that the expression of 2 Cor 8:23 means
that the apostles are a reflection and revelation of the
exaltation of Christ? His divine power and glory are manifest in church and world in the apostolic office.[11]

3. Theological reflection, it is true, especially the scriptural exegesis of Evangelical theology, poses us now a
question about certain decisively important expressions of
the Lord. Understood according to our frequently presented exegesis, they no doubt establish priestly ministry
in the church. But the question is whether such expressions
and commissions are directed to a real and special priestly
class in the church, and not rather to the whole priestly
church, so that authority and discharge of the ministry
would be a matter of the church's collective responsibility.
We reach a deeper insight into the biblical expression when
we admit this question.

[11] The expression then recalls Jn 17:22: "The glory which you
[Father] have given me I give to them." This too says that the
disciples, who remain in the world after the departure of the Lord,
make his divine glory present to the world.
If it is natural enough in 1 Cor 11:7 for Paul to say that the
husband is "God's image and glory," then it is still much more
natural for him to say this of the apostle. See also 2 Cor 3:18,
where however the interpretation of κατοπτριζόμενοι is not unanimous.
Does Paul say that we mirror back the glory of the Lord or that we
behold the glory of the Lord?

Actually, the Lord's expression: "Everything that you bind on earth will also be bound in heaven" (Mt 18:18) stands in the context of a general instruction for disciples. Matthew 18 represents one of the oldest institutions of the community. The task of binding and loosing is awarded to the disciples, thus to the whole church. The group of disciples will be represented in individual instances by the assembly of the community, led perhaps by apostles or bishops. But this is not essential. Rather it is the church as a whole which is committed to care of souls. The church is to fulfill this commission by profession of faith, by acting in communion, by ministry in love (Heb 13:15f), by intercession (Rom 1:9), by sacrifice of self (Rom 12:1). To all it is said in behalf of all: "Build up one another" (1 Th 5:11).

The celebration of the supper was apparently carried on from the outset in the circle of the Twelve, and they were first to receive the commission: "Do this in memory of me" (Lk 22:19). The apostles themselves saw to the observance of this commission as well as of others (see above, 105f). But this commission still assuredly belongs to the whole church. Therefore to the present day no priest is supposed to celebrate Mass without at least a Mass server to represent the communion of the co-celebrating church (according to the *Codex Juris Canonici*, canon 813, § 1). And the celebration of the Sunday Mass of the community is called in German the "Office," or the "High Office" (*Hochamt*), certainly not as office of the celebrant, but as office of the whole community. The word of teaching and preaching at divine service is also a commission on all. Paul says to the church of Corinth assembled for divine service: "When *all*

speak in prophecy and there enters an unbeliever or non-
initiate, then he is convinced by all, judged by all. The
secrets of his heart become manifest. He falls on his face
and prays to God and confesses that God is really in your
midst" (1 Cor 14:24).

The baptism-mandate too is spoken in the narrowest
circle of the apostles (Mt 28:19). Yet it has always been
understood in the church as a commission which not only
the apostles have been empowered to execute, but every
individual man as well. Therefore the commission to preach
the gospel, which was united to the baptism-mandate, also
holds true precisely not only for the narrowest circle of
apostles, but for the church.

We shall not want to dispute the church's possession of
the priestly dignity, which it has as a whole and which each
of the faithful has; it is our duty to proclaim that dignity
and the commission which it contains. The church and
each of its faithful mediates salvation to the world. But
there is truth to be recognized in the other sayings of the
Lord and of the apostles which tell that the apostles are
selected from the band of disciples and immediately sent
out by Christ. For the church is built up on them (Eph
2:20), and presbyters as well as bishops have been appointed by the spirit (Acts 20:28). According to this testimony, it is by the apostolic office that the word of the
church is announced in an authoritative manner and its saving and sanctifying will brought to the world in a special
manner.

The fathers too, in accord with the teaching of the Bible,
knew the priestly dignity of the whole church. Although it
was especially the earliest of them who constructed its

hierarchy, even these nonetheless emphasize the unity of the classes of the church. According to Ignatius of Antioch and Cyprian, the church exists in the bishop and the bishop in the church. The bishop is not the church, but its plenitude, just as, conversely, the people are the plenitude of the bishop (Ignatius, To the Trallians 3:1; Cyprian, Letters 33:1; 66:8). Augustine interprets the saying about the primacy (Mt 16:18) thus: "So Peter alone does not loose, but the whole church together binds and looses sins. . . . We too have the keys. You too bind, you too loose. For whoever has been bound is separated from your communion, and whoever is separated from your communion is bound by you; and when he is released, he is loosed by you, because you too pray God for him" (Commentary on the Gospel of John, PL 124:5). As late as the high middle ages, there is evidence of a consciousness that the sacraments are not discharged only by office holders in the church, but that the intercession of the church is included as an element of the sacramental action.[12]

Once more in our own day there is the powerful entreaty of Pius XII in his encyclical Mediator Dei that this teaching be renewed. The encyclical, citing an expression of Innocent III, says that "the whole church joins in the eucharistic oblation made by Christ and offers sacrifice with him." The pope goes on to say that "the faithful present the sacrifice not only by the hands of the priest, but in a certain measure with him. By this sharing, the oblation of the people itself is taken up into the liturgical cult."

Neither among the charismatics nor among the other

[12] See F. X. Arnold, Glaubensverkündigung und Glaubensgemeinschaft, 1955, 111–113.

office holders does the New Testament name any ministers
of the church with the ancient and hallowed word ἱερεύς
(priest). At any event, it employs words which point to
priestly ministry, as when it speaks of a "priestly working"
(ἱερουργεῖν) of the apostle (Rom 15:16) or of his "cultic
ministry" (λατρεύειν: Rom 1:9), or when it calls him liturgos
(λειτουργός: Rom 15:16; see Phil 2:17). But Tertullian is
first to call the bishop once summus sacerdos (On Baptism
17); Hippolytus speaks once (Refutation of Heresies 1:6)
of the highpriesthood (ἀρχιερατεία) of the apostles. Eusebius
(History of the Church 10:4, 2) is first to address the
clerics as ἱερεῖς in his festival address.

But at any rate, the New Testament emphatically employs the words "priest" and highpriest," ἱερεύς and ἀρχιερεύς,
of Christ, who is presented here as the one priest and highpriest of the new covenant (Heb 2:17; 4:14, et al). The
true liturgy is his in commission (Heb 8:2, 6). For this
reason he is, according to 1 Tim 2:5, the one, unique
mediator: "One is God, and one is the mediator between
God and men, the man Jesus Christ." But the Apocalypse
(1:6; 5:10; 20:6) repeatedly calls the faithful "priests for
God," while 1 Pt 2:5, 9 calls the church a holy and royal
priesthood.

This leads us back to the start of our considerations. We
proceeded from the fact that the priesthood is ascribed to
the church in the First Letter of Peter. What this general
priesthood signifies and contains is not unimportant. The
whole church shares in discharging the sacraments (see
above, 128f). All have a part in the priestly dignity. If the
apostles are bearers of the spirit and the spirit works on the
church by their office, still it is all the faithful originally

who are endowed with the spirit, all who are "spiritual men."* This is what Paul says in one passage after another. The spirit is what makes the Christian, so that whoever did not have the spirit would be no Christian (Rom 8:9). But now God's spirit dwells in us, and now "we all have been given to drink of one spirit" (1 Cor 12:13). Each has been given also his own gift of the spirit for ministry in the church (1 Cor 12:7). It was in the time of Constantine that the monks and clerics first began to designate themselves simply as "spiritual men" in contrast to lay people. We said that the apostle mediates God's word in the word of proclamation; yet, according to 1 Th 4:9, *all* the faithful are *immediately* "instructed by God." Cultic consecration bestows knowledge: "You have the anointing of the Holy One, you all have knowledge. . . . His anointing instructs you about everything and is true; there is no lie in it" (1 Jn 2:20, 27). Indeed the group of disciples preserved a saying of the Lord which so thoroughly integrated the teacher into the group of brothers that a special title and class was simply no longer allowed the teacher, lest the one teacherhood of the Lord be obscured: "You are not to let yourselves be called teacher. For one is your teacher; you are all brothers" (Mt 23.8f). Therefore all have the duty of giving witness (1 Cor 14:26; Ap 12:11). The whole church is a cultic community. This is also expressed with considerable force in the New Testament's frequent designation of the church as God's holy temple (1 Cor 3:16f; 2 Cor 6:10; Eph 2:21),

* *Geistliche:* the German expression is a noun (spirituals) used to designate priests and ministers, equivalent to the English "men of God."

and the Christians generally as the saints, that is, those consecrated for cult. Paul ascribes to the whole church the commission and dignity, by simply being what it is, "to present to God a living, holy, and well-pleasing sacrifice in a spiritual divine service" (Rom 12:1). The charitable action of the church of Philippi he calls "a sacrifice of good odor, a sacrifice of love, pleasing to God" (Phil 4:18). Therefore Paul is "poured out as libation in the sacrifice and liturgy of the church's faith" (Phil 2:17). Thus the whole church offers sacrifice and celebrates priestly ministry. According to Heb 13:15f, the whole church brings God the sacrifice of praise and of charitable deeds. In Tit 2:3, the women are advised to live as ἱεροπρεπεῖς, in a way that befits a holy place, indeed "in a priestly way."[13] The cultic ministry, which Rom 1:9 ascribes principally to the apostle, is often accorded to all the faithful as their task (Lk 1:74f; Phil 3:3; Tit 2:3; Heb 12:28). In the magnificent liturgical visions of John's revelation (Ap 7:15, 22.3) the *ecclesia triumphans* continues the cult which it has already been celebrating as the *ecclesia militans*.

The history of religion likes to seize upon such passages to show that old cultic notions and representations have undergone a spiritualization in them.[14] This is certainly true. The material sacrifices have been put aside. But that the

[13] As in M. Dibelius, H. Conzelmann, *Die Pastoralbriefe*, 3rd. ed., 1955, 104. [The phrase in Titus is ὡσαύτως ἐν καταστήματι ἱεροπρεπεῖς: literally: "as if suited in condition for the sacred"—tr.]

[14] Often quoted to this effect is H. Wenschkewitz, "Die Spiritualisierung der Kultusbegriffe Tempel, Priester, und Opfer im Neuen Testament," *Angelos* 4, 1932, 71–230. See Ph. Seidensticker, "Lebendiges Opfer," *Neutestamentliche Abhandlungen* 20, 1/3, 1954, 17–43.

cult has been spiritualized does not mean that all cult has been put aside and abolished. The New Testament pronouncements on the cult of the church are not to be understood as merely figurative. They are pronouncements on a cult which is true and real even when the sacrifice and cult are called "spiritual," that is, sacrifice and cult given reality by the spirit (Rom 12:1; 1 Pt 2:5; Heb 13:15), and therefore never autonomous human achievement. Indeed in the New Testament "spiritual" does not mean something figurative or improper or unreal; a spiritual reality is the strongest of realities anywhere, namely the reality that fulfills with divine spirit and life, a reality therefore more real than all merely human and earthly realities.

Now it is becoming completely clear in what sense there is an individual priesthood in the New Testament, and why the New Testament ascribes the old word "priest" to none of the office holders of the church. The original holders of apostolic office as well as the later ones who replace them fulfill mediative-priestly ministry in word and deed. If the New Testament nevertheless does not call them "priests," then the reason for its not doing so is that this word, determined in its content by the history of religion, could be misunderstood at first, as if it meant that an individual could be a priest in the church—in the sense in which the priests of the heathen and of Israel were priests, who in an independent ministry of their own traded between earth and heaven, prophesied by divination, and offered cultic sacrifices.

The apostolic church maintained exactly the same attitude toward the word ἱερός (sacred). Just as the linguistic feeling of the Septuagint already shunned the word, the New Testament too almost entirely avoided it (the single exception being 2 Tim 3:15*). The word was so full of heathen religiosity that it was found unemployable by both the old and the New Testament. Therefore the word ἅγιος was used by the Bible. It is only in keeping with this precise linguistic sense that the Greek Old Testament, for example, almost never calls the temple in Jerusalem τὸ ἱερόν—for Judaism distinguished its house of God from the heathen temples—while the New Testament was capable of designating both Jewish and heathen temples as τὸ ἱερόν. For in the New Testament view the Jewish place of cult was something of the past, so that there was no longer any point to distinguishing the Jewish from other sanctuaries. But when the New Testament speaks of the new temple, especially of the spiritual temple of the church, it almost always employs the word ναός, which word in the Septuagint characterized the sanctuary of Israel.[15]

Thus, avoiding the unemployable word ἱερεύς, the New Testament introduced its own designations of offices. For this, young Christianity took up words previously little used, words which had not yet taken on any definite character or content, words that had at any rate no religious-cultic connotation as yet; then it attached these words to the new offices of the church. Some of them passed again out of use (such as ἡγούμενος and προϊστάμενος); others be-

---

* A reference to the ἱερὰ γράμματα of the Old Testament.

[15] At any rate, the Septuagint employed the word ἱερεύς, apparently because no other was available for designating the priest. See the lexicographical evidence of G. Schrenk in *Theologisches Wörterbuch zum Neuen Testament*, vol. 3, 221–247.

came set designations such as διάκονος, πρεσβύτερος, ἐπίσκοπος)
and passed into the modern languages as foreign words or
borrowed words. The words διάκονος and ἐπίσκοπος the church
took over from Greek usage, the word πρεσβύτερος from
(Hellenistic) Judaism. When we meet them in the New
Testament, we must at times consider how we should
translate them. Are we to render διάκονος as "helper" or as
"deacon," πρεσβύτερος as "elder" or as "priest," ἐπίσκοπος as
"superintendent" or as "bishop"? At all events, there is
reason for generally rendering διάκονος as "deacon" and
ἐπίσκοπος as "bishop," because these designations in the New
Testament already clearly are concerned not merely with
individual performances of service, but with enduring
offices, precisely the new offices of the church. But may
πρεσβύτερος be translated as "priest"? This translation too
must be allowed, since the word was used within Judaism
and outside it in a formal manner as a title without regard
to the age of the one so designated, and the New Testament
usage leaves no doubt that the presbyters were so named by
no means because of their advanced age. In the New Testament the word does not designate a chronological classifica-
tion, but an occupation in the community.[16] Thus the translation "elder" would not actually be suitable. According to
the Acts of the Apostles (14:23, 20:17), Paul appoints
presbyters in his place when he leaves a community. Also,
according to the pastoral letters (Tit 1:5), presbyters are
in charge of office in the communities. Perhaps, since noth-

[16] See W. Michaelis, op. cit. 47f (where, to be sure, it is said
that the word πρεσβύτερος in its translation as "priest" has gone
through "a complete transformation of its content"); M. Dibelius,
H. Conzelmann, op. cit. 60f; C. Bornkamm in Theologisches
Wörterbuch zum Neuen Testament, vol. 6, 651–683.

ing is said about presbyters in the older letters of Paul, one
might question whether this institution was already in force
by Paul's time. Still, the testimonies we have seen show that
in any event this was the way the community was constituted as early as the first century—namely that the leaders
of the church in such communities were presbyters. Without detriment to the apostle's continuing supreme pastoral
right, the presbyters have to carry out the ministry which
the apostle himself has carried out previously (Acts 20:28).
If his service was priestly, then so also is theirs. Therefore
the translation of πρεσβύτερος as "priest" is fully justified for
the Acts of the Apostles and the pastoral letters. According
to Jas 5:14f, the presbyters certainly also carry out priestly-
mediative ministry in the anointing of the sick, in that
they do a saving work by discharge of sacramental action.

The church is united with God and will always be united
with him anew by the priesthood of Christ, who has consecrated the whole church to share his priestly ministry.
There can be an individual priesthood only insofar as it
participates in the priesthood of Christ, represents this,
and makes it present in the world. An individual priesthood
always belongs to the priesthood of the total church. This
being so, there is nothing in the New Testament to indicate
that a general and a special priesthood would be in any
way opposed to each other. They are a joyful fellowship.
Thus, those who call themselves and who are called priests
are not to forget that the brothers and sisters are a priestly
and royal generation which has entered the sanctuary with
them. "We designate all Christians as priests, because they
are members of the one Priest" (Augustine, City of God
20:10).

6 FOLLOWERS IN THE OFFICE OF APOSTLE

"CALL THE PRIESTS OF THE CHURCH" (JAMES 5:14)

Priests and bishops are not apostles. The apostles have been given their vocation by the Lord, have seen the resurrected Lord, and have been sent out by him himself. They alone can claim to have been sent "not by men and not through men, but through Jesus Christ" (Gal 1:1). The church is "built on the foundation of the apostles and prophets, with Jesus the cornerstone" (Eph 2:20). On the twelve foundation stones under the walls of the celestial Jerusalem stand the names of the twelve apostles (Ap 21:14). For all time the church remains bonded to the initial apostolic word and testimony. Therefore the time of the apostles has as the apostolic age its unique meaning for the history of the church. All this constitutes the single unrepeatable dignity and meaning of the apostles. To this extent their office is untransferable.

But the apostles themselves selected assistants whom they sent out as representatives; and the apostles, when they had to leave a church behind, appointed in their place superintendents of the communities. These provisions and adjustments arose naturally from the needs that occurred in the church's development. How the apostles regarded these is attested typically in the case of Paul and his work by writings of the New Testament of various origins. Paul sends forth his pupils Silvanus, Timothy and Titus in his stead and commands that they be accepted as he himself would be accepted who sends them. For Timothy prepares for the work of the Lord as Paul himself does (1 Cor 16:10). The proclamation of Paul and his co-workers is the same (2 Cor 1:19); they minister the gospel in the same manner (Phil 2:22). Paul and his co-workers have one and the same Spirit (2 Cor 12:18).

Paul admonishes the church in Thessalonica to acknowledge those "who labor for the community, superintend it in the Lord, and admonish it, and to hold them in high esteem for the sake of their work" (1 Th 5:12f). At Philippi Paul has left behind bishops and deacons, who superintend the community in the apostle's absence and in his behalf, even though he himself has retained the supreme authority (Phil 1:1). Paul presumes superintendents in the Roman church, with which he was not personally acquainted (Rom 12:8). He knows of a "deaconship for the saints" (1 Cor 16:15), to whose authority the fellow members of the community owe attention and obedience. Both Paul and the church know and esteem the "charisms of government" (1 Cor 12:2, 8). According to the testimony of Acts 20:17–35 on the constitution of the communities at the time of the apostles, the church is led by men who are called presbyters at one time and bishops at another. Since Paul has to leave his community behind, they are to pasture the flocks over which the Holy Spirit has set them, as Paul has done. 1 Peter 5:1–4 admonishes the presbyters to pasture the flock of God entrusted to them as they ought to do. In this passage the ministry of the successors is designated with the same terminology and imagery as was used for the first apostle, when it was said: "Pasture my lambs, pasture my sheep" (Jn 21:15–17). According to the Acts of the Apostles and the pastoral letters, it is a matter of set institution that Paul, the first apostle, appoints superintendents of the churches who are called bishops, presbyters and deacons, and who are to continue the activity of the apostle. Therefore ministry and authority of teaching are transferred to the superintendents, and they will hand on their office in their turn (1 Tim 1:3; 4:11). The letter already sees the line of tradition unfolding which will continue through the successive ages of the church: "You, my child, be strong in grace in Christ Jesus; and what you have learned from me before many witnesses, entrust this to reliable men who are capable of teaching others in their turn" (2 Tim 2:1f). The superintendents, as the apostles before them, have the right to establish order and to lead: "I have left you behind in Crete for this purpose, that you make arrangements for whatever still needs to be done and appoint presbyters in every city as I have commissioned you to do" (Tit 1:5). If however the ministers and superintendents of the communities are set up by imposition of hands and prayer (Acts 14:23; 1 Tim 4:14; 5:22; 2 Tim 1:6; see above, 98f), then the gesture of imposition of hands does indeed mean that the one who imposes his hand intends to pass on the authority that he himself holds by right. Here the prayer expresses the consciousness that in the enactments of man it is God who makes the election and produces the effect, and that human action is validated by this fact (2 Tim 1:6). Therefore the Acts of the Apostles (20:28) is capable of saying of the bishops who have been appointed by men that the Holy Spirit has appointed them.

Surely it is in keeping with the intention of the New Testament that the assistants of the apostles and the office holders who later replace the apostles are to serve the church and lead it, as the apostles have done: they have the same plenitude of divine endowment and power as the apostles had, and, following the human model of the apostles, they have the same manner of administration and government.

In the synoptic gospels too there is an implicit indication that the church considered the apostles an example which obligated the following generations of missionaries and community leaders. For there can be little doubt that a writing as early as the great missionary discourse which lies before us in chapter 10 of the Gospel of Matthew is not intended by the evangelist merely to narrate a single instance of sending missioners out. While the discourse narrates the earlier mission of the apostles, the gospel intends to give to the missionaries of its own time directions for their ministry, which they are to carry out as the apostles were to carry out theirs.

Thus in all this the New Testament says that apostolic ministry continues to live and work in the commissioning of priests and bishops of the church.

But still another vocation and another office continues

to work in the ministry of the priests and bishops. The *Didache* (15:1) says this clearly: "Choose for yourselves bishops and deacons—men, worthy of the Lord, gentle, free of avarice, truthful, and proven. For they too make available to you the ministry of the prophets and teachers. Therefore do not pay them scant heed. For they are men of honor among you together with the prophets and teachers." The *Didache* names in prophets and teachers two of the classes of vocation and spiritual endowment attested in the New Testament. These two stand for all. Many of them are enumerated in 1 Cor 12:28: "Apostles, prophets, teachers, those empowered with miracles, gifts of healing, the work of charitable assistance, governance, speaking with tongues." The offices of the spirit are taken up in post-apostolic times into offices of the church's hierarchy. Therefore, in the institution of these offices and in the institution of laws, it is power and manifestation of the spirit that must predominate. Every office of the new covenant is a ministry of the spirit. From this every office receives its glory: "How should the ministry of the spirit not be glorious?" (2 Cor 3:8).

If only the office holders of the church knew and understood under what vocation and obligation they serve and live: to guard and even to increase the heritage of the apostles and prophets.